BEFORE YOU QUIT
A Marriage Counseling Handbook

EMMANUEL ELENDU

Copyright © 2017 by Emmanuel Elendu

Before You Quit
By Emmanuel Elendu

Printed in the United States of America

ISBN: 10: 0996459014
ISBN: 13: 978-0-9964590-1-3

All rights reserved. No part of this book may be reproduced, stored in retrieval system, or transmitted in any form or by any means: electronic, mechanical, photocopies, recording, scanning or other-except for brief quotations in critical reviews or articles, without the prior written permission of the publisher. This book or parts thereof may not be reproduced in any form, stored in a retrieval system, or transmitted in any form by any means- electronic, mechanical, photocopy, recording, or otherwise- without prior written permission of the publisher, except as provided by the United States of America copyright law. Unless otherwise noted, all Scripture quotations are from the New King James version of the Bible. Copyright © 1979, 1980, 1982 by Thomas Nelson, Inc., publishers Used by permission.

Cover Design By: Faith Walley

Published By:
Cibunet Publishing
P. O. Box 444
Woodlawn, NY 10470
Email: admin@cibunet.com
Website: www.cibunet.com

Table of Contents

DEDICATION: 7

FOREWORD: 8

CHAPTER 1: 11
First Get it Right with God
Lesson 1: Seeing the Big Picture
Lesson 2: Man is Subject To Change and Decay
Lesson 3: Man must see the way God sees

CHAPTER 2: 35
Marriage: Locating your niche
Family: Something must be fishy
Something has changed in our time!
Marriage: The way you see it
The African Marriage: A Synopsis
Marriages in India
The Western Marriage
Marriage: The way God sees it

CHAPTER 3: 69
Marriage in a Cross Cultural Setting
Marriage in Plain Language
Marriage and Cultural Considerations
The Other Way that Causes Pain
An African-American Cultural Mismatch

An Indian Overture
In Brazil Ladies shop for Husbands

CHAPTER 4: 85
Hosea Beeri & Gomer Diblaim
A Marriage Example
The Hosea in your Marriage
"Yes I do"

CHAPTER 5: 101
Money Matters & Divorce Issues
Where it all started
Adam's Configuration
Financial Management
Wealth Creation
Wealth Management
Remembering the Good Times
What factors are associated with a higher risk for divorce?
How Common is Divorce and what are the reasons for it?
If You Quit
The Turning Point

REFERENCES: 150

Dedication

To my love, my friend and my wife, Chinwe

Foreword

Today, statistics show that the divorce rate among Christians is at the same level as non-Christians. Both clergy and laity alike are abandoning marriage relationships for the slightest provocation or for even minor excuses which may be resolvable.

Marriage is no longer held in high esteem in the western world today as it was in time past. A famous preacher here in North America said this to justify her divorce from her husband; "If I bought a Cadillac and no longer want it, I simple sell it and buy another." Well, that is the new attitude of many towards holy matrimony in our society.

There is also mainstream philosophy which redefines marriage in such a way that legalizing bestiality will soon become proposed legislation in many states and ultimately an issue for the courts to resolve. We cannot leave the current besiegement of the marriage union to chance and that is what prolific author Pastor Emmanuel Elendu has boldly confronted in this book.

There are principles that serve as a foundation for a godly marriage that lasts the test of time. From the premarital relationship through the wedding and marriage proper, there are vices we must guide against and virtues that we must uphold in order to enjoy marriage. Learning through experience only, is too costly and may result in a regrettable divorce. If you can be equipped through knowledge to avoid a divorce, why not?

Understanding the cross-cultural challenges that beset not only marriages of those from different cultural backgrounds, but also those who migrate from their place of origin and settle in foreign societies is crucial to be able to hold steady the rudder of the marriage. Pastor Elendu addresses various cultural scenarios that play out in the multi-cultural environments that may influence some of the decisions of players in a marriage union and how to manage such.

I believe that 'Before You Quit' is a must read for anyone planning to marry or is already married or even separated or contemplating a divorce.

Dr. Kenneth Walley
President of KWI and Overseer of New Faith Tabernacle Churches.

Chapter .1.

FIRST, GET IT RIGHT WITH GOD

He stood strong; stoutly built from the muscles of his frame. He was a missionary to the core; ready to go; and preach at any moment; I mean any moment. His zeal amazes the piety and his energy (in the Lord) sends a cold shrill on the Bishops of our day; thinking whether they have been called into the same work force as my friend, Mr. El Yak. Indeed I feel liturgical and bizarre at the ooze from his unction. My friend had come from his city to obtain visa to go to United Kingdom for a sponsored Master of Art (MA) in Theology. As we paced to the door of my apartment in Mafoluku, Lagos; Yak fixed his passionate gaze at me... "What is it, brother? I inquired. With a deep sigh, he said; "Papa Elendu, if I had known that this is how it's going to be in this marriage, I would have called it off a day to my wedding. No! I if I had known one hour to the wedding; no, an hour is too long. If I had known that this is what it would look like, a second to the wedding I would have called it off. Truly God knows that I mean what I am saying" "Stop that, please stop that. Don't make such confessions, brother" I rebuked. "Hmmnnn, let us go into the house. I will tell you why" he muted with quivering, shaky lips.

That night was a tale of woes and worries. It was a night of prayer and talks. We hoped things got better. El Yak had married a year prior his visit to the British Embassy. I was a part of his train and we were colleagues in the ministry; 1988 through 1990. Yak was passionate about his call to preach the gospel; his wife was passionate about him going out there to make some big money, though she was gainfully employed. There was always this "fight" at home and argument around ministry; that the 'head of the house' ought to bring in the cash. El was deficient of cash, but rich in grace and compassion. This cross road was a hard one to travel. When El gained a full ride (scholarship) into one of UK's highly prized schools of Theology to further his career, he was merely wasting his time, courtesy of his wife. As we talked, a message went to British Embassy from the spouse (being a British citizen) that her husband should be denied the visa, though fees had been paid by the sponsoring organization. El was asked by the Embassy to go home, resolve whatever differences he had with his wife. That MA dream in Europe was aborted and El then enrolled in a School of Theology in Jos, Nigeria. You can bet he was not a happy man but did his best to keep head above the waters; doing ministry and taking care of immediate and extended family members. El Yak was on his way driving to the Plateau City of Jos, with the barrage of thoughts on his mind or was it that he slept off; sped into a standby tree; there he died.

Before you draw conclusions, may I ask you to pray that the good Lord will help you navigate the tortuous waters of life, especially, your marriage and grant you grace and wisdom to come ashore with good results to show. May I ask you who are unmarried to begin to pray for your life partner, where ever he is, whoever he or she may be. First, we want to establish that the marriage we intend to discuss in this book is the type ordained by God as written in the Bible. Marriage is between a man and a woman (for in the beginning God made them male and female, and in the likeness of God He made them, male and female). The union between man and woman was ordained by God right from the beginning for God declared that it is not good for man to be alone, and thus He created woman for him (Adam) that they may have fellowship together, and that they may worship together and procreate on Earth. These are, in part, reasons why marriage was instituted. It is therefore out of the law of God and His purpose to assume celibacy and pretend that marriage is not to be desired and worked. It is honorable; marriage is wholesome and complete and good, as ordered by the owner of heavens and earth. Whatever may have happened to the union and the covenant, whatever may have been declared 'permissible' and allowed to sweep through the isles; whatever shift and turn marriage has taken, it is hoped that God will restore in our homes and society. As civil society redefines marriage and evil creeps into the heart of men and women to think that the woman and the man can live separately without the other; or the same sex living together in the guise of equal opportunity and liberty of expression, has to be fixed by the Church.

To portray a home as one that contends with difficulties without the father or one with many children with different fathers and mothers paints an ugly picture of what God intends from the beginning. Marriage remains a picture of things to come; of the relationship between Christ and His Church. Marriage and the home remains the tool in the center of God's outreach to the world. In this book, we intend to discuss reasons behind the "whys" in marriage pitfalls as we take a long peep into the picture spread out before us in the holy writ. To the best of available information, we will discuss different cultures and how they mix with the West's interlock; then we will introduce the final word on the issue from the Bible. Someone said that most marriages suffer because of financial strain and disagreements. We will look into this as well and prefer solutions towards fixing this problem. To the extent a man and a woman are willing to go the long haul and see marriage as 'work' and mutually beneficial to each other; as God's assigned mission field on Earth, to the extent both will sail ashore in the canoe of marriage. We will uncover some myths with counsel from the Book of life and proffer suggestions based on research and godly wisdom from the elders of our community. Let us get started with big lessons that underlie life, generally.

Lesson 1: Seeing the Big Picture

If I forget the ultimate, I will be enslaved by the immediate.
- John C. Maxwell

The chief purpose of life in time is to gain merit for life in eternity.
-St. Augustine

I know you have seen many a Christian marriage fallen apart, and you have also observed the once-upon-a-time professing Christian brother or sister throw away the very basic idea of one-man-one-wife doctrine from the apostles to embrace the homosexual stain. I have also seen many with successful stories and a balanced presentation of the doctrines of Jesus Christ. These come to us with a big question as to what is happening to the faith delivered to us in its pure and undiluted form. I want to assume that you are born again and filled with the Holy Spirit; that Christ is being formed in you on a daily basis and there is no draught of grace in your life. I want to also believe that as we go through this manual, you will be very open to yourself and to the Lord to discern through your heart and purpose for marrying and make a definite determination of what He intends for you and your marriage. As you know and have been taught by many preachers, no marriage is perfect. Everyone is a work in progress and so, as we all build together, there is need for counsel and admonition and encouragement.

One thing that kept my focus in ministry and marriage are some things I want to share with you, so they form the bedrock for our discussion. They are revelations from the Lord about where I am going and the ultimate for engaging in Christ's call to follow the narrow and strait path. The big picture is the glory and the 'well done' of the Father. It is paradise;

the heavenly home; the place of rest where Jesus sits and rules the heavens and the earth. A revelation and a glimpse of the glory to come demean and distils all earthly encumbrances and weights as nothing. In ministry, when a man sees heaven, sees the glory to come or understands from scriptures what is ahead and the blessedness of the call; then everything and anything become ephemeral, disdained and ordinary.

In life, what we see determines how we move, react or behave. Or what we price highly and where our drive and passion rest. It determines where our treasures are laid; our purpose in life and its pursuit. What you do vent your energy on tell us a great deal of what you are seeing. Your sight (eye) is your gateway in life. So we may pause to ask "what do you see?" What has been revealed to you about life and where you are going? Until a man or woman understands life and what it is all about; he/she picks the nuggets of heaven and the fellowship God ordained to fill marriage; the man or woman may substitute the fellowship with something else. That something (the main pursuit); when it fails or is absent, there you find problems and issues in marriage. Again, what is your big picture? What do you see? What is the purpose (a continuous constant that drives your passion) in marriage? I urge you to see the BIG PICTURE and align your focus; making sure your treasures are well laid. When you see the big picture, everything falls in its proper place.

WHAT DO YOU SEE?

Repeatedly in Scripture, God asked several persons this question: "What Seest Thou?" "What do you see?" Jeremiah: (1:11, 13; 24:3), Amos: (7:8; 8:2), Zechariah: (4:2; 5:2), Do you see...? Prov.22:29; 29:20, Abraham: Do you see...? Jas.2:22

Depending on the answers they gave, God often said, "You have seen well" We too must see well.

What you see determines your view of eternity and this determines how you go about earthly business including marriage. Marriage, seen from periscope of meeting the obligations of bearing children only hits a deadlock when God withholds babies from coming out of the marriage or; even when kids come; the excitement about your spouse is gone because you have 'used' her or him to achieve your expectation. If the big thing behind your view of marriage is beauty; when beauty begins to wane and wither, your energy about your spouse is also diminished. If it is sex, the day you are denied sex, that day marriage begins to suffer a setback. If the big picture is on money and how much he can bring home, the day there is cash squeeze, then problem arises.

So whatever it is that forms a big picture before you or that occupies the centre of your understanding of marriage or drives the intention; will drive the whole marriage and define the ultimate relationship you keep with your spouse. As we list what we see and where our drives and passions are pointing to, we must make a serious determination what it is that we see and drive towards. I pray that you may see something bigger than what is physical, bigger than the picture the world has painted for you and cling to the eternal things; to the glories revealed - our end and home above. My prayer is that you understand the heartbeat of God and begin to see Jesus in your spouse as a partner; to discover a colleague with whom you have been assigned to travel the road to heaven. As we walk, hands and hearts joined, as we work (yoked), that the Lord may appoint us the grace to see in one another, a candidate with whom we must take to heaven together (without whom, it may be almost impossible, by reason of the yoke, to get to the gate of heaven). So, again may I ask "What do you see...in your spouse?"

Sometime in 2002 a young pastor was talking to me about his estranged wife: "She is a witch, she wants to kill me. You do not understand who I am talking about. She is a witch and there is nothing I can do with her" I refused to understand with him, though I never met with his wife. I told him I was ready to fly over to Europe to see the wife and we would begin to mend any broken relationship. I knew God can change any heart and fix any kind of problem. To begin such a fix, my friend must begin with a refresh on the concept of his wife; to see some mission field in the wife; a vessel Christ Jesus died for and rose again; that even if she is a witch, God can still deliver completely, all those who have been entrusted into His care. My friend saw a 'witch' and went further to rename his wife a witch. What you speak into the air forms into a 'being' as a result of the power of the tongue. So it will be absurd to call your spouse names and expect the best out of the person; instead, we should bless with our tongues. Again I ask, "What do you see?" Can you inquire from the Lord to show you something bigger than you thought? We are all limited by sight. You need to see something more glorious; something bigger than what you see presently.

Lesson 2: Man is Subject To Change and Decay

Among all the things that lead to divorce and separation, the major cause is money; then abuse, lack of respect and love; among many others. As Ephesians chapter five puts it succinctly, the roles of husbands and wives are to be exemplified with or mirror the relationship between Christ and the Church.

I learn from the passage that as Church changes in the different dispensations, so does man change. As a woman makes overtures and is given to flavours and flowers, so does the Church. As there is little depth in discernment in man or woman to the point that every wind of doctrine carries them away, so is the Church (sometime I am afraid to call it spiritual adultery). These are the inevitable traits of man. He is always changing. There you find Christ Jesus, never changing. There also lies the mystery: that an unchanging God can come down to relate with a changing man and even gave His life for a mere man. Man, as you know, is weak and fragile; limited and contained in a vessel called Body. He is subject to death and decay. God is everything, the opposite...and yet He came down in the likeness of man, to relate and live with man.

> "And that he died for all, that they which live should not henceforth live unto themselves but unto Him which died for them and rose again"
> 2 Corinthians 5:15

"Husbands, love your wives, even as Christ loved the Church and gave Himself for it" Ephesians 5:25

This is fully loaded. Can mortal man fulfil these demands "...**even as Christ loved the Church...**" Naturally speaking, that is impossible. With God, it is possible. As a man, you may bask in euphoria that male dominance and control is a legal, unscripted code of conduct that resonates with and gains heaven's approval. That may be culturally enshrined. The Bible states that there should be mutual relationship. "**Submit yourselves one to another in the fear of God.**" Ephesians 5:21 and also the scripture admonishes wives to "**submit yourselves unto your own husbands, as unto the Lord**" and "**for you husbands, love your wives, even as Christ loved the Church and gave Himself for it.**"

It takes the love of Christ to love "even as Christ loved the Church" It therefore takes one who has been and seen Jesus Christ; being changed into His likeness; to love a wife as Christ loved the Church in the face of all the demands, the nagging, the vulnerabilities we find with women. Suffice to say that that is the way women are made. By survival instincts, they most often do what men call names; they are just the way they are created. A close look at the Manufacturer's manual (the Bible) you will find the resemblance with the Church. In the midst of all these, the husband must love his wife... even as Christ loved the Church, and gave Himself for it.

I found it very difficult to come to terms with dying for my would-be wife as a teenager. It made no sense to ask a young man to yields his neck for death where it was needed because of a wife. This passage was a tough one for me and so I decided I was not going to marry. It was until I found the truth about "grace" and God's ability in a man; then I began to reconnect again. I received a life-line. I discovered that to be able to die for my wife, I must first be dead to self, sin and Satan. 'Death' is the key word here. It all started with the death of Jesus Christ on the Cross of Calvary. It was for the very purpose of dying that Jesus came to the world. As Simeon held this baby Jesus in his arms, he declared "...and a sword will pierce through your soul, you are set up for the rising and fall of many..." Why death at a baby's dedication that should be filled joy and excitement? The dew of death from Calvary comes down on every useful life consecrated to the Lord. The same applies to marriage. The pangs of death grip a man and; he really dies. Until this death occurs, there may not be any meaningful fruitfulness heaven recognises in your life or marriage.

Death to self and death to sin must occur. Then when Satan comes with tricks and treats, you will be bold to tell him "I am already dead, there is no place for you to occupy" At this point you begin to live in Christ Jesus; you begin to find true meaning in what Christianity and Christian marriage is all about.

> "If ye then be risen with Christ, seek those things which are above, where Christ sits on the right hand of God. Set your affection on things above, not on things on earth. For ye are dead, and your life is hid with Christ in God... Mortify therefore your members which are upon the earth..." Colossians 3:1-5

Death must work in a man or woman for the scriptures to be fulfilled in that life. The reason is that until a corn of wheat falls to the ground and dies, it remains alone and unfruitful. But when it dies it decays and is dismembered; without 'a self-worth' or any personality. The heat of the earth comes hard on it, living organisms begin their work of scavenging and moisture incubates with the heat until it dies. Soon after death, it begins a new life, it sprouts, and it blossoms. (John 12:24-26)

As Henry F. Lyte (1793-1847) had his last communion with his congregation arising from a long history of ill-health, he wrote the song later that evening before he expired:

Abide with me! Fast falls the eventide;
The darkness thickens. Lord with me abide.
When other helpers fail, and comforts flee,
Help of the helpless, O abide with me!
Swift to its close ebbs out life's little day;
Earth's joys grow dim, its glories pass away;
Change and decay in all around I see;
O Thou who changest not, abide with me!
Not a brief glance I beg, a passing word;
But as Thou dwell'st with Thy disciples, Lord,
Familiar, condescending, patient, free
Come, not to sojourn, but abide with me.
Come not in terrors, as the King of kings,
But kind and good, with healing in Thy wings,
Tears for all woes, a heart for every plea,
Come, friend of sinners, and then abide with me.
Thou on my head in early youth didst smile;
And though rebellious and perverse meanwhile,
Thou hast not left me, oft as I left Thee,
On to the close, O Lord, abide with me!
I need Thy presence every passing hour.
What but Thy grace can foil the tempter's power?
Who like Thyself my guide and stay can be?
Through cloud and sunshine, O abide with me!

I fear no foe with Thee at hand to bless:
Ills have no weight, and tears no bitterness.
Where is death's sting? Where, grave, thy victory?
I triumph still, if Thou abide with me.
Hold Thou Thy cross before my closing eyes;
Shine through the gloom and point me to the skies;
Heaven's morning breaks, and earth's vain shadows flee!
In life, in death, O Lord, abide with me!

When a man is conquered he will be able to love his wife as Christ loves the Church. The conquered man must have been conquered by heaven and sees only the things that have eternal significance. Otherwise you will see a man whose life is wrapped around himself, the world and all the shows. That man holds tight to earthly things and his life is directed by the things he sees.

> "You haven't seen a selfish man until you've seen a man who sees no heaven, has no vision, no room for sacrifice, has a tight grip on material possession and draws strength in numbers"

Lesson 3: Man must see the way God sees

When God 'produced' man (Adam), He had something in mind. He added woman (Eve). He made the heavens and Earth and looked at the whole thing and found that they were good and in excellent working condition. But as sin got into the whole mix, the Earth was denatured. His 'products' have manufacturer's manual for reference fixing. The word of God, the Bible, is God's (Manufacturer's) manual for everything and anytime fixing. Depending on the reader's inclined thinking and education, both earth and man have their dysfunctional frame from the hit the prince of this world threw at them. As these happened, God took note; had this to say:

"Lord, in the beginning you made the earth, and the heavens are the work of your hands. They will disappear into nothingness, but you will remain forever. They will become worn out like old clothes, and some day you will fold them up and replace them. But you yourself will never change, and your years will never end" Hebrews 1:10-12 (TLB)

"And again to the Son, You, Master, started it all, laid earth's foundations, then crafted the stars in the sky. Earth and sky will wear out, but not you; they become threadbare like an old coat; You'll fold them up like a worn-out cloak, and lay them away on the shelf. But you'll stay the same, year after year; you'll never fade, you'll never wear out" Hebrews.1:10-12 (The Message)

"Lift up your eyes to the heavens, and look upon the earth beneath: for the heavens shall vanish away like smoke, and the earth shall wax old like a garment, and they that dwell therein shall die in like manner: but my salvation shall be forever, and my righteousness shall not be abolished" Isaiah 51:6

"Every good and perfect gift is from above, coming down from the Father of the heavenly lights, who does not change like shifting shadows" Jas.1:17 (NIV)

Charles Spurgeon declared, "All that Nature spins time will unravel, to the eternal confusion of all who are clothed therein."

God is pointing to the pervading change that afflicts all creation. As man boasts of his achievements, his wealth, his fame and professionalism; he forgets about the decay before him. He thinks less of the recorded playback of his life and his ordeal with his spouse. He is limited in understanding. Following is the way God sees man, thinks about the Earth and all its show and tell.

DIFFERENCES IN VIEWPOINTS OF GOD AND MEN

The World (Man's viewpoint)	God's Ruling
A. From Luke 16:15 • Highly esteemed (KJV) • Highly valued (NIV) • Important (CEV) • Important (GW) • Monumental (Msg) • Attractive • Wonderful	A. From Luke 16:15 Abomination Detestable Worthless Disgusting Monstrous Repulsive Trash
B. From 1Samuel 16:6-7 Samuel: "Here he is! God's anointed!" Msg	B. From 1 Samuel 16:6-7 God: I've already eliminated him.

The World (Man's viewpoint)	God's Ruling
1. But the LORD said to him, "Pay no attention to how tall and handsome he is. I have rejected him, because I do not judge as people judge. They look at the outward appearance, but I look at the heart." TEV	1. But the LORD said to him, "Pay no attention to how tall and handsome he is. I have rejected him, because I do not judge as people judge. They look at the outward appearance, but I look at the heart." TEV
2. But GOD told Samuel, "Looks aren't everything. Don't be impressed with his looks and stature. I've already eliminated him. GOD judges persons differently than humans do. Men and women look at the face; GOD looks into the heart." Msg	2. But GOD told Samuel, "Looks aren't everything. Don't be impressed with his looks and stature. I've already eliminated him. GOD judges persons differently than humans do. Men and women look at the face; GOD looks into the heart." Msg
3. But the LORD told Samuel, "Don't look at his appearance or how tall he is, because I have rejected him. God does not see as humans see. Humans look at outward appearances, but the LORD looks into the heart."	3. But the LORD told Samuel, "Don't look at his appearance or how tall he is, because I have rejected him. God does not see as humans see. Humans look at outward appearances, but the LORD looks into the heart."
4. But the Lord said to Samuel, "Don't judge by a man's face or height, for this is not the one. I don't make decisions the way you do! Men judge by outward appearance, but I look at a man's thoughts and intentions." TLB	4. But the Lord said to Samuel, "Don't judge by a man's face or height, for this is not the one. I don't make decisions the way you do! Men judge by outward appearance, but I look at a man's thoughts and intentions." TLB

The World (Man's viewpoint)	God's Ruling
5. But the LORD said to him, "Take no account of it if he is handsome and tall; I reject him. The LORD does not see as man sees; men judge by appearances but the LORD judges by the heart." NEB	5. But the LORD said to him, "Take no account of it if he is handsome and tall; I reject him. The LORD does not see as man sees; men judge by appearances but the LORD judges by the heart." NEB
6. But the LORD said to Samuel, "Don't judge by his appearance or height, for I have rejected him. The LORD doesn't make decisions the way you do! People judge by outward appearance, but the LORD looks at a person's thoughts and intentions." NLT	6. But the LORD said to Samuel, "Don't judge by his appearance or height, for I have rejected him. The LORD doesn't make decisions the way you do! People judge by outward appearance, but the LORD looks at a person's thoughts and intentions." NLT
C. From Revelations 3:14-22 Laodiceans: (Laodicea means "Judgment of the people") You brag...You say...	C. From Revelations 3:14-22 Jesus: (The Faithful and Accurate Witness, Rev.3:14, Msg) Do not realise and understand...Knowest not that... "I know you inside and out, and find little to my liking. You're not cold, you're not hot--far better to be either cold or hot!

The World (Man's viewpoint)	God's Ruling
I'm rich, I've got it made, I need nothing from anyone, Increased with goods Have need of nothing I have prospered and grown wealthy I have need of nothing I don't need a thing! With everything I want	You're stale. You're stagnant. You make me want to vomit. Oblivious that in fact you're a pitiful, blind beggar, Threadbare and homeless. Wretched Pitiable, Pitiful Blind Miserable
D. From Revelations 2:8-11 Smyrna:	C. From Revelations 2:8-11 Jesus: "I can see your pain and poverty--constant pain, dire poverty--but I also see your wealth
Poverty Tribulations and suffering Afflictions, distress and pressing trouble Prison	But really you are rich! (Heavenly riches, TLB); Crown of Life Be faithful unto death (not, "You're under a curse") It won't last forever!

Translations used above: The Message (Msg), Amplified, The Living Bible (TLB), KJV, NIV, Good News Bible (TEV), God's Word, New Living Translation (NLT), Contemporary English Version (CEV), New English Bible (NEB).

"Be God's fool – that's the path to true wisdom. What the world calls smart, God calls stupid. It's

written in Scripture, He exposes the chicanery of the chic." 1 Corinthians.3:19 (Msg)

I think it really hurt God to undo what He did and watched over it, saying, "This is good." It will be heart breaking for any parent to pull a son or daughter through college with all fees paid for while the son on graduating, turns his or her back on the parents. Marriage is honorable and good. It should not be entered into unadvisedly.

Chapter .2.

MARRIAGE: LOCATING YOUR NICHE

Dr. Arinze Ikemme is a great friend whose story lines give me much of inspiration. On one occasion he ministered at the Dayton Ohio branch of the Church where he told a story that has stuck with me for years. I went further, inquired about same story just to find that a similar style has been published. Here's what Dr. Ikemme shared:

That's One
During a widely televised interview between a man and his wife in their 50 year old marriage, they

claimed that there has never been an argument or a quarrel. The anchor man was quite surprised and wanted to know the secret. He asked the man, "Please tell us the secret to this perfect harmony in your home"

"On the way to our honeymoon after courtship, we decided to take our horses through the beautiful mountain passes of Europe. As the horses were crossing a small stream, my wife's horse misstepped and jostles over my horse. As we rode across the stream, my wife dismounted from her horse, walks over to the horse, and stares into his eyes. Sternly and irritated as she looked, finally she says, "That's one." She remounted her horse and we continued our ride.

A bit further down the path, my wife's horse stumbles again when he tried to step over a fallen tree. Again, my wife dismounted, stares the horse in the eyes, and irritably, fuming with anger, tells the horse, "That's two!" She returned to saddle her horse and we moved on. As the afternoon sun began to set, my wife's horse once again lost his footing on a mossy, mesh slope. My wife dismounted, moved to the horse, and helped her horse out of contact with any of us, then moving to the front of the horse she stares him direct in the eyes and firmly shouted, "That's three." Then she pulled her pistol from her vest, and shot the horse dead.

I was quite upset at seeing the beautiful horse killed and I said to my wife, "That's terrible, why would you do such a thing?" She stares at my face and irrevocably said to me, "That's one!" Since then there has never been an argument between the two of us.

Family: Something must be fishy

Family building blocks are needed in these times as the enemy has exercised himself in undoing the very thing God instituted. In Genesis chapter one verse twenty-six, God said, let us make man in our image; and in the likeness of God man was made, patterned after his Maker, man therefore inherited the DNA of God the Father, God the Son and God the Holy Spirit. As fellowship continued in Eden between man and God, there was this vacuum that nothing else could fill. Remember, God was there for Adam, they talked, they reasoned together. I can imagine God coming in the cool of the evening to say, "hello son, how's the day been? how did you come up with such wonderful names for all the animals and birds and trees, and ... (as though He was not the One who supplied the names, initially)?" In a way, God had real fun with Adam.

But in the midst of all activities and labor, Adam was lonely. "It is not good for man to be alone, I will make for him, a help, suitable for him" was God's response to the need that echoed back to the throne of grace. Eve was created for Adam.

Thank God He did not create Adam and Steve neither did He make Eve for Evelyn. It was Adam (the man) and Eve (the woman). So anything outside this protocol amounts to rebellion and an invitation of God's wrath on the fellow who so chooses to defy the order.

In Genesis chapter two verses 15, 16 and 17 there God gave Adam instruction on how to run the garden. Most times the Lord gives the man instructions on how the home should run (supplement or support can come through the woman) the man being the head of the home receives the order from God. Anything contrary is an aberration of God's law. The center is out of joint in that case.

So Adam was working, fully engaged in labor and having fun in Eden; though lonely. It is a wholesome privilege for a man to do something to fend and to provide for the home, no matter how small. Call it the pride of man. God approves that! **He that finds a wife finds a good thing and obtains favor of the Lord!** I suppose Adam was lost in labor, in naming those animals and birds and trees and... He was consumed in the Lord's work. As the Lord saw this, it grieved Him that His son was very lonely. Nobody to say, "welcome honey, my love" "how was today's job?" So God fanned him to sleep. Remember Adam was busy in the Lord's appointed vineyard. It tells me there is a pattern to "finding a wife." First be on fire for God. Let His business on earth consume your desire and your passion. Get involved, and that deeply, in the house of God! Second, as you labor and pray, look up to God. To find, you first "sleep off" if God must be allowed to guide you, make a choice. For Adam, he slept. It is against nature and heavenly protocol for a lady to go to a man and ask his hand in marriage. Virtue has lost its meaning in such a circumstance. Ichabod is on display! (the glory of the woman must have departed). So Adam slept. Mr. man, are you willing to sleep? Can you call on your God in the name of His Son, Jesus Christ, to choose for you? Not all in skirts and blouses qualify for the high calling as wives! **Eve was created: beauty personified, charming and loving, tender to hold and to behold.** As Adam opened his eyes from sleep, there was this chasm that caught his eyes. I think he lost his count and was awed in suspense. "Waaaaooooh she shall be called Woman!" There is something that 'waaaooooed' you when you dated your wife. Those waaaoooh moments must be restored today. Strike the original match again, get back on course and start off again.

    Suffice to mention that many women are not enjoying this embrace and so they turn sour and cranky. The twists and turns in life squeeze the juice out of them. Hence they become 'woe' to the man. They are lions and tigers at home. The man is afraid to come back to his base, his kingdom where he is supposed to preside as 'king'. He's been made a horse that is used whenever needed. Not so sister! Your facial expression, your words should waaaooooh the man; your embrace should send him to sleep. Remember you are a help, made suitable for him.

Genesis 2:24&25, "...and the man shall leave his father and mother and shall cleave to his wife and they shall be one flesh. And they were both naked, the man and his wife and were not ashamed." Assuming as a man, you still receive directives on how to run your home from your parents, you've some serious issues. You must leave them and cleave to your wife. And the two were naked, not ashamed of one another. Nothing is hidden, not your salary, not your stocks and bonds, not your estates, not your bank account. No sickness is hidden, Nothing! You are in the boat together...on the high sea. It is until death, do you part. Amen

Something has changed in our time!

The seeming twist in values and ethical health checks take their cues from a grand design by proponents of satanic doctrines to institutionalize programs of the antichrist, the beast; in an angular style towards Armageddon. Whether it is in the Church with emphasis on money, fame and power, or Politicians with their drive towards enabling deep rooted soul-search for Power (which crystallizes into amassed wealth and money); not to mention in other spheres of life where the common denominator remains money; these leave us with the conclusion that Family is after-all, under the weight of a chief definer: Cash/Money. Family then is up for sale!

There is a 'FOR SALE' sign on the door of every FAMILY! The highest bidder steals the show and buys the air wave, begins his/her propaganda. The once committed son of a priest, the politician (or even the Clergy), considers his electorate and his quest to remain in office, sells his conscience and changes his mind on family as consisting of man and wife; to board the train of homosexuals, the gay or lesbian rights movements and the law to uphold their unholy marriages. It was Billy Graham who said, "If God does not judge us in this generation for all these, then He owes Sodom and Gomorrah an apology."

Some fussy ideologies believe that there are no absolutes; everything is subjective and follows chance events and outcomes... (Remember Charles Darwin?). But we know God is the creator of the heavens and the earth. He spoke them into being. He created (made man and woman in His image, after His likeness, just like Himself) and gave instructions to Adam and Eve (Genesis 1:2:25-28). These activities are basic absolutes, took place in the Garden (the Euphrates of today). But like a headless train heading for destruction, man has plumaged into some illusion and arrogance to stamp God out of his psyche; to silence his conscience forever. Reverend Akinola, speaking in Canada at the Convention for Arch-Bishops of the Anglican Communion, succinctly declared against gays and lesbians: "...even dogs cannot do what you are proposing, they know the course of nature; they fear God." No wonder God has chosen to give up on them, to allow for this end game since constant, continuous rebuke has been issued, unheeded to. (Hosea 4:7; Romans 1:18-22; Revelations 20)

According to the American Psychiatric Association (APA), until 1974 homosexuality was a mental illness. Freud had alluded to homosexuality numerous times in his writings, and had concluded that paranoia and homosexuality were inseparable. Other psychiatrists wrote copiously on the subject, and homosexuality was "treated" on a wide basis. There was little or no suggestion within the psychiatric community that homosexuality might be imagined as anything other than a mental illness that needed to be treated. Of course, homosexuality was listed as a mental illness in Diagnostic and Statistical Manual of Mental Disorders (DSM-II). Then in 1970 gay activists protested against the APA convention in San Francisco. These scenes were repeated in 1971, and as people came out of the "closet" and felt empowered politically and socially, the APA directorate became increasingly uncomfortable with their stance. In 1973 the APA's nomenclature task force recommended that homosexuality be declared normal. The trustees were not prepared to go that far, but they did vote to remove homosexuality from the list of mental illnesses by a vote of 13 to 0, with 2 abstentions. This decision was confirmed by a vote of the APA membership, and homosexuality was no longer listed in the seventh edition of DSM-II, which was issued in 1974.

Philip Hickey, one respected writer had this to say in his paper "Homosexuality: The Mental Illness That Went Away." "What's noteworthy about this is that the removal of homosexuality from the list of mental illnesses was not triggered by some scientific breakthrough. There was no new fact or set of facts that stimulated this major change. Rather, it was the simple reality that gay people started to kick up a fuss. They gained a voice and began to make themselves heard. And the APA reacted with truly astonishing speed. They realized intuitively that a protracted battle would have drawn increasing attention to the spurious nature of their entire taxonomy. So they quickly "cut loose" the gay community and forestalled any radical scrutiny of the DSM system generally."

Among the 55% of the members of the DSM (which was by no means unanimous) who voted, favored to forestall the scrutiny of their system. Of course, the APA put the best spin they could on these events. The fact is that they altered their taxonomy because of intense pressure from the gay community, but they claimed that the change was prompted by research findings. So all the people who had this terrible "illness" were "cured" overnight – by a vote! Real illnesses are not banished by voting or by fiat, but by valid science and hard work. Since then, the war against FAMILY has continued to rage. As you know, give the devil an inch, he takes a yard; grant him a yard, he goes for a mile... It is interesting that homosexuality does meet the APA's present criterion for a mental illness! This criterion is:

"... A clinically significant behavioral or psychological syndrome or pattern that occurs in an individual and that is associated with present distress...or disability...or with a significantly increased risk of suffering death, pain, disability or an important loss of freedom." (DSM-IV-TR, p xxxi)

It could be argued that mental and psychological conditions for gay people have improved considerably since 1974, (thanks to medical research and administration) but they are still subject to close spiritual examination and attention. Any group or individual who opposes the institution of MARRIAGE (One man, One woman prototype) is roaming in the evil forest. They are the Church's big assignment in our communities. Vocal as they seem to be, there remains a void, a call for mercy and intervention into a dysfunctional psyche. Anyone who strays from the Designer's original manual (Matthew 19: 5-12; Genesis 1:25-28) and way of operation is mentally retarded and must be helped.

This leaves us with the real question as a Church: In our Show-and-Tell of a FAMILY, how do we present this holy institution to the people out there? What is the content and flavor we bring to "lure" these dysfunctional folks into the institution? There seems to be a mix of cultures (forcing African tradition in an American/European setting); of values; a clash of interests (divergent interests and schemes of spouses). In a time where divorce is cheap, the courts turning out significant sum from fillings of same, what really drives you nuts to head towards the courts and seek solace from one who makes his money off of your depravity? Check it, it is selfishly motivated. You can bear the hurt and love him or her to death. Because the kids are unruly and mom and dad are constantly engaged in a fist, those outside this institution have nothing to emulate. They see the HOLY Institution of marriage a trivial contract that has lost its value over time. They spurn at it because the custodians have despised this revered ordinance. Think about the change you'd bring to the table; the flavor humanity is waiting for in your neighborhood; the grace and glamor marriage and family bring to society. Say something; go, do something!

You are the light of the world; the world is looking for this light... Shine in the midst of darkness. Shine; shine; shine! Marriage must be preserved. It is God-ordained; nature upholds it...even the dogs, cats all approve that, "He made them male and female" ... in the beginning. As Dr. James Dobson in "Focus on the Family" broadcast would always say, "Let's turn our heart towards home."

Marriage: The way you see it

Your definition of marriage or expectations that formed your concepts and ideas around it are definitely not a conclusion made in a single short. It culls from years of exposure and teaching and practice. Like any project, to get it executed with the right skill-set and toolkit, there must first be a definition of the business process, then a crafting of the requirements to meet stakeholders expectations and fulfill desired business direction and overall business plan and purpose; then you begin a design strategy. In the Information Technology (IT) world, the design and build stages of a system's evolution are dependent on the business case definition. In marriage, the definition you hold or you were taught will be your base line, your guiding light, as it were. How do you see marriage? What do you hope to get out of it? Who taught you marriage? These are the basic questions we must address in this chapter.

The African Marriage: a Synopsis

The African culture teaches marriage to be likened to a man as the boss, the lord of all; whose words and commands are final. The man is the center of all things. Women are taken as maids; helpers when needed and tools for sex and children bearing. After the traditional marriage, some cultures put the woman in a 'fattening room' where she is fed with good foods and never to work for months. She is prepared for the man. There, the women accept that culture and live with it. They do not speak where men are, are confined in the kitchen when important family matters are discussed. The man may marry as many wives as he can afford and once the bride price is paid, the woman leaves father and mother into the ma's house; the man having full responsibility and liability over the woman.

The man must work 24/7 to fend for the family and see to it that the woman is well fed, clothed and sustained; whatever it takes to do that. The man is the bread winner; he is the provider of the butter and over sees all things that touch on financial responsibility. The man enjoys doing that; never complaining. It is a thing of pride. Suffice to say that it is the parents of the woman who decide for her on who to marry; (they choose a man for her); so from the beginning the woman has no opinion, no adjudication over her life nor an add-on to the turns or framework her life takes as she grows. Because the woman is not culturally the winner of bread or expected to win any, she is most of the time, not educated, not exposed to skill-sets that stand her out or provide opportunities for growth, economically; after all, she will be confined at home, cooking food, keeping the home and raising children. This is, in part, the African culture before Christianity and development found its way into the shores of the continent.

Marriages in India
Arranged marriages have been part of the Indian culture since the fourth century. Many consider the practice a central fabric of Indian society, reinforcing the social, economic, geographic, and the historic significance of India (Stein). Prakasa states that arranged marriages serve six functions in the Indian community: (1) helps maintain the social satisfaction system in the society; (2) gives parents control, over family members; (3) enhances the chances to preserve and continue the ancestral lineage; (4) provides an opportunity to strengthen the kinship group; (5) allows the consolidation and extension of family property; (6) enables the elders to preserve the principle of endogamy (Prakasa). The practice of arranged marriages began as a way of uniting and

maintaining upper caste families. Eventually, the system spread to the lower caste where it also was used for the same purpose. The specifics of arranged marriages vary; depending on if one is Hindu or Muslim." Marriage is treated as an alliance between two families rather than a union between two individuals" (Prakasa). Ninety-five percent of all current Indian marriages are arranged, either through child marriages or family or friend arrangement. The Child Marriage Restraint Act of 1929-1978 states that the legal age for marriage is 18 for females, and 21 for males, with most females being married by 24 and most males being married by their late twenties (McDonald). However, many children, age 15 and 16 are married within a cultural context, with these marriages being neither void or voidable under Hindu or Muslim religious law, as long as the marriage is not consummated until the legal age of 18 for females and 21 for males.

Muslim Arranged Marriages in India
In the Muslim faith, it is the responsibility of the parents to provide for the education and the marriage of their children. The parent's duties are not considered complete unless their daughter is happily married (Ahmad). Marriage is a Sunna, an obligation from the parent to the child that must be fulfilled because the female is viewed as a Par Gaheri, a person made for someone else's house. In this

custom, it is the responsibility of the groom's parents to make the initial move toward marriage: seeking eligible females and insuring their son is marketable. Once a female has been selected, the father of the male sends a letter to the perspective bride's father, through a Maulvi, a liaison between the families, asking the father if his daughter can marry his son. If the female's father accepts by letter, then a formal ceremony is held at the female's house, where the father of the groom asks the girl's father can his daughter marry. A feast and perhaps the giving of gifts, depending on the region of the exchange, follow the "asking" ceremony. During the feast, the respective parents set a time to solemnize the marriage, "usually during the summer season (garmiyan) because it allows more time for people to attend". The date of the actual marriage ceremony depends on the age of the individuals, which ranges from four years to eight years after the "asking" ceremony (97). Most Muslim arranged marriages are solemnized four years after the "asking" ceremony.

 The ceremony itself consists of a sub ceremony: the maledera, where female members of the male's family wash and dress the male in traditional clothing, and the female dera, where the female is washed, given henna, and given ceremonial jewelry. The actual marriage ceremony (nikah) consists of both individuals being asked if they agree to marry. Once a yes is acknowledged, the Koran is read, and the father determines a dowry, with 40% being paid at the nikah and an agreement that the rest will be paid later. The paying of a dowry is culturally optional, but legally unlawful. Once the dowry has been agreed on, a marriage contract is drawn up and the girl goes to live with the spouses's family. If the daughter remains unmarried, she is considered a spinster, who brings shame upon her family, and she is considered a burden. A woman also suffers this fate if she is separated or single past 24 years old (Stein).

Hindu Arranged Marriages in India

Marriage is a sacramental union in the Hindu faith. "One is incomplete and considered unholy if they do not marry" (Parakasa). Because of these beliefs, many families begin marriage preparation well in advance, with the help of "relatives, friends, and 'go-betweens'". Most females are married before puberty, with almost all girls being married before 16, while most boys are married before the age of 22 (Gupta). However, couples normally do not consummate the marriage until three years after the marriage ceremony. The legal age for marriages is 18 for females and 21 for males (Mc Donald). The male's family is responsible for seeking the female. "A majority of Hindu marriages take place outside of their home village." The man's family is responsible for arranging the marriage. Like Muslim arranged marriages, the Hindu culture uses a matchmaker to help find possible matches. Once a match is found and arrangements met, the two families meet to discuss dowry, time, and location of the wedding, the birth stars of the boy and girl, and education (McDonald). During this time, the males of the family huddle in the center of the room, while the perspective couple sits at the periphery of the room and exchange glances. If the two families agree, they shake hands and set a date for the wedding (McDonald).

Most Hindu pre-wedding ceremonies take place on acuta, the most spiritual day for marriages. The ceremony often takes place early in the morning, with the male leading the female around a fire (punit) seven times. After the ceremony, the bride is taken back to her home until she is summoned to her husband's family house. Upon her arrival, her husband's mother is put in charge of her, where she is to learn the inner workings of the house. During this time she is not allowed to interact with the males of the house, because she is considered pure until the marriage is consummated. This period of marriage can range from three to six years (McDonald).

Arranged Marriage Matchmaker in India
The traditional arranged marriage matchmaker is called a nayan (Prakasa). The matchmaker is

normally a family friend or distant relative who serves as a neutral go-between when families are trying to arrange a marriage. Some families with marriageable age children may prefer not to approach possible matches with a marriage proposal because communication between families could break down, and could result in accidental disrespect between the two families (Ahmad 68). Matchmakers can serve two functions: marriage scouts, who set out to find possible matches, and as negotiators, people who negotiate between families. As a scout and negotiator, a family sends the nayan into the community to seek possible matches. The matchmaker considers "family background, economic position, general character, family reputation, the value of the dowry, the effect of alliance on the property, and other family matters" (Prakasa). Once a match is found, the matchmaker notifies his or her clients and arranges communication through him or her. Communication is facilitated through the nayan until some type of agreement is met. Depending on the region, an actual meeting between the families takes place, to finalize the marriage agreement, while also allowing the couple to see each other.

Once a marriage agreement is met, the nayan may be asked to assist in the marriage preparations: jewelry and clothing buying, ceremonial set-up, and notification of the marriage to the community (Ahmad). The nayan usually receives no pay for his or her services, but may receive gifts: clothing, food, and assistance in farming from both families for the services they provide. Newspapers, the Internet, television ads, and social conventions serve as the modern nayan (Prakasa). Indian families in metropolitan cities use the mass media as go-between as a way of bridging cultural gaps, in areas where there may be a small Indian population.

Dowries in India

Dowries originally started as "love" gifts after the marriages of upper caste individuals, but during the medieval period the demands for dowries became a precursor for marriage (Prakasa). The demand for dowries spread to the lower caste, and became a prestige issue, with the system becoming rigid and expensive. The dowry system became a tool for "enhancing family social status and economic worth" (61). Prakasa notes five purposes of the dowry: (1) provides an occasion for people to boost their self-esteem through feasts and displays of material objects; (2) makes alliances with the families of similar status; (3) helps prevent the breakup of family property; (4) gets a better match for daughters; (5) furnishes daughters with some kind of social and economic security (61-62). The expensive nature of dowries has helped raise the marriage age in the middle and lower caste because families have not been able to meet dowry demands, and has also forced some families "to transcend their caste groups and find bridegrooms from other sub caste and different caste."

There are some disadvantages to dowries. Families may suffer financial hardships due to the expensive nature of dowries. They may not be able to afford dowries, therefore prohibiting their children from marriage, causing "girls to occasionally commit suicide in order to rid their fathers of financial burdens." Because of social instances like these, many consider "the dowry system as a social evil and an intolerable burden to many brides' families."

As a result, the Dowry Prohibition Act of 1961 was passed. It decrees, "to give, take, or demand a dowry is an offense punishable by imprisonment and fines". A dowry is also defined as "any property or valuable security given or agreed to be given either directly or indirectly by one party to a marriage to the other party to the marriage, or by the parents of either party to a marriage or by any other person, to either party to the marriage or to any other person at or before or after the marriage as consideration for the marriage of the said parties" (Diwan). The law does make the following exclusion: "any presents made at the time of marriage to either party to the marriage in form of cash, ornament, clothes or other articles, do not count as a dowry." These items are considered wedding gifts. The law does create the following loop hole; "the giving or taking of dowry does not affect the validity of the marriage, if the dowry is given, the bride is entitled to it, but the person giving it is punished by law if discovered."

In some sense, the African and Indian traditional marriages are similar and portray same traits as funded by the holdings of the man and extended family members.

The Western Marriage

In the United States there have been three basic marriage models: The historic Judaic-Christian marriage model, the Romantic marriage model, and the Rationalistic marriage model. The historic Judaic-Christian model has roots deep within Jewish tradition. This model views marriage as a very special gift from God that should be used for man's benefit. By taking care of his spouse and living life the way God intended for man to live, man therefore serves God. According to this model, a man and woman experience a very special bond through marriage. Though not commonly referred to as a sacrament by American Protestants, Roman Catholics commonly refer to marriage as a sacrament. The Judaic-Christian model believes that the institution of marriage is a creation of God and that the couple is joined as one by God. The purpose and function of marriage in this model is to have companionship, to love each other, and to help one another with the daily struggles of everyday life. The second purpose is to have children and be an outlet for sexual expression.

In 2003 there was the debate over whether to allow same-sex access to the institution of civil marriage became a major political issue, due to these important court decisions:

"June 26, 2003: The U.S. Supreme Court rules that antigay sodomy laws violate the U.S. Constitution's right to privacy."

"November 18, 2003: The Massachusetts's Supreme Judicial Court rules that denying marriage to same-sex couples violates the state's constitutional guarantees of equal protection and due process." Same-sex marriage is currently legal in 19 states: Massachusetts since May 17, 2004, Connecticut since November 12, 2008, Iowa since April 24, 2009, Vermont since September 1, 2009, New Hampshire since January 1, 2010, New York since July 24, 2011, Washington since December 9, 2012, Maine since December 29, 2012, Maryland since January 1, 2013, and New Jersey since October 21, 2013, in Hawaii since December 2, 2013, New Mexico since December 19, 2013, Oregon since May 19, 2014, Pennsylvania since May 20, 2014, Illinois since June 1, 2014, as well as in the District of Columbia since March 3, 2010 and Eight Native American tribes. Utah briefly performed same-sex marriages from December 20, 2013 to January 6, 2014. Michigan performed same-sex marriages on

March 22, 2014. Same-sex marriages were also briefly performed in Arkansas and Wisconsin. Laws vary because marriage laws are the purview of individual states. The 1996 Defense of Marriage Act prohibited the federal government from recognizing these marriages until its third section was struck down by the U.S. Supreme Court on June 26, 2013 in United States v. Windsor. The social movement to obtain the right of same-sex couples to marry began in the early 1970s, and the issue became prominent in U.S. politics in the 1990s.

Massachusetts has recognized same-sex marriage since 2004. Nine states and the District of Columbia offer same-sex legal unions that offer some or all the rights and responsibilities of marriage, but these rights are not automatic with civil union as a result of a federal statute. In contrast, twenty-six states have constitutional amendments explicitly barring the recognition of same-sex marriage. Forty-three states have statutes restricting marriage to two persons of the opposite sex, including some of those that have created legal recognition for same-sex unions under a name other than "marriage." A small number of states ban any legal recognition of same-sex unions that would be equivalent to civil marriage.

State anti-miscegenation laws banning interracial marriage date as far back as the 1660s. These laws were gradually repealed between 1948 and 1967. The U.S. Supreme Court declared all such laws unconstitutional in Loving v. Virginia in 1967. Polygamy is "a condition or practice or culture of having more than one spouse". The United States is seen as a monogamous nation (a nation where polygamy is a criminal offense). About 100,000 people practice polygamy secretly and illegally. These are the marriage formats people have been taught or come to live with on a daily basis. If we see marriage from these perspectives, then there is definitely going to be problems with man and woman living together. Because there is a way God sees marriage, a way He put marriage together, then I think He is the final authority on the book on marriage. God laid the basic foundation of marriage. When it was too difficult for the Israelites to cope with issues around marriage, they insisted that Moses would provide a panacea as a way of escape out of the mayhem called marriage. Moses did. And further in the century, the Pharisees confronted Jesus to ask his opinion for the same reason their fore-fathers permitted a written note of divorce for a 'not-too-wonderful' relationship to be broken and part ways.

Marriage: The way God sees it
"The Pharisees also came to Him, tempting Him and saying unto Him, Is it lawful for a man to put away his wife for every cause? And He answered and said unto them, Have ye not read that He which

made them at the beginning made them male and female; and so this cause shall a man leave his father and mother and shall cleave to his wife and they shall be one flesh. Wherefore they are no more twain but one flesh. What therefore God hath joined together, let no man put asunder" Matthew 19:3-6

Man's / Woman's view Point	God's Standard
1. Marriage is falling in love, having fun and all the good stuff from my spouse	The Lord caused a deep sleep to fall on Adam... out of his ribs He formed a woman
2. It is a contract between two people	It is a covenant between man, the wife and God. Malachi 2:14
3. Marriage is your responsibility to make it work. I am doing you a favor	"That is why a man leaves his father and mother and is united with his wife, and they become one. The man and the woman were both naked, but they were not embarrassed" Genesis 2:24,25
4. If mama isn't happy, no one will be happy. Everything must be done to satisfy me, myself and I.	"Be kindly affectionate to one another with brotherly love, in honor giving preference to one another; not lagging in diligence, fervent in spirit" Romans 12:10-13 NKJV

Man's / Woman's view Point	God's Standard
5. I am looking out for another horse to ride and when I get one, I shall kick you out in the cold	"Who can find a virtuous woman? for her price is far above rubies. The heart of her husband doth safely trust in her, so that he shall have no need of spoil. She will do him good and not evil all the days of her life. She seeketh wool, and flax, and worketh willingly with her hands". Proverbs 31:10-13 KJV
6. You go make money, bring it home	"She is not afraid of the snow for her household: for all her household are clothed with scarlet... She maketh fine linen, and selleth it; and delivereth girdles unto the merchant" Proverbs 31:21, 24
7. My mother is preferred to any woman	"Because we are members of His body; That is why a man leaves his father and mother and is united to his wife, and they become one flesh" Genesis 2:24(NIV); This mystery is great; but I am speaking with reference to Christ and the church.... Ephesians 5:31, 32

Man's / Woman's view Point	God's Standard
8. I married you to help pay my bills and so cut the monthly check for me.	"For it is a good thing that the heart be established with grace; not with meats, which have not profited them that have been occupied therein" Hebrews 13:9
9. I am marrying you because my parents asked me to.	Whosoever that finds a wife finds a good thing and obtains favor of the Lord Proverbs 18:22
10. I love him, so I am going to marry him no matter what; I will pay my way through	The man said "This is now bone of my bones and flesh of my flesh she shall be called 'woman' for she was taken out man" Gen. 2:2 NIV; "And in that day seven women shall take hold of one man, saying, we will eat our own bread and wear our own apparel, only let us be called by thy name, to take away our reproach" Isaiah 4:1
11. My ministry comes first, then my marriage; for I have a high calling from God and I must fulfill it	"A bishop then must be blameless the husband of one wife, vigilant sober, of good behavior, given to hospitality, apt to teach; Not given to wine.." 1 Timothy 3:2-12 KJV

Man's / Woman's view Point	God's Standard
12. Marriage should not come between my money and my spouse. It is my hard earned money. She/he can go and make her/his money. Mine is mine.	Then the Lord God placed the man in the Garden of Eden to cultivate it and guard it. 16 He told him, "You may eat the fruit of any tree in the garden, 21 Then the Lord God made the man fall into a deep sleep, and while he was sleeping, he took out one of the man's ribs and closed up the flesh. 22 He formed a woman out of the rib and brought her to him. 23 Then the man said, "At last, here is one of my own kind - Bone taken from my bone, and flesh from my flesh. "Woman' is her name because she was taken out of man." Genesis 2:15,16,21-23
13. The woman is made for man, so whenever I need sex I should have it	"Submit yourselves to one another because of your reverence for Christ" Ephesian 5:21 "Do not deny yourselves to each other, unless you first agree to do so for a while in order to spend your time in prayer; but then resume normal marital relations" 1 Corinthians 7:5-15

Man's / Woman's view Point	God's Standard
14. Because whoever that does not provide for members of his household is worse than an infidel so I must build a house first for my parents, train my siblings and carter for my relations before engaging in any major project in my home.	"But she that liveth in pleasure is dead while she liveth... but if any provide not for his own and specially for those of his own house hath denied the faith and is worse than an infidel" 1Timothy 5:6; 8
15. Marriage is for procreation; I will therefore have sex with you and be sure that you can have children for our home before I commit to it.	"Marriage should be honored by all and the marriage bed kept pure for God will judge the adulterer and all the sexually immoral" Hebrew 13:4
16. I can marry anytime, anywhere, whoever I want; it is my life.	"Abraham was now a very old man, and the Lord had blessed him in every way. 2 One day Abraham said to his oldest servant, the man in charge of his household, "Take an oath by putting your hand under my thigh 3 Swear by the Lord, the God of heaven and earth, that you will not allow my son to marry one of these local Canaanite women. 4 Go instead to my homeland, to my relatives, and find a wife there for my son Isaac." Genesis 24:1-4

Man's / Woman's view Point	God's Standard
17. Whatever he earns is ours, my money, my wealth and properties belong to me. He is the head of the home.	She brings him good, not harm, all the days of her life; she selects wool and flax and works with eager hands. She is like the merchant ships, bringing her food from afar, she gets up while it is still dark, she provides food for her family and portions for her servant girls. She considers a field and buys it out of her earnings she plants a vineyard" Proverbs 31:12 - 16

Man's / Woman's view Point	God's Standard
18. My wife is a nice woman but the beautiful ones are yet unborn. These girls look cute and really beautiful.	"My son, attend unto my wisdom, and bow thine ear to my understanding: That thou mayest regard discretion, and that thy lips may keep knowledge. For the lips of a strange woman drop as an honeycomb, and her mouth is smoother than oil: But her end is bitter as wormwood, sharp as a two edged sword. Her feet go down to death; her steps take hold on hell. Lest thou shouldest ponder the path of life, her ways are moveable, that thou canst not know them. Let thy fountain be blessed: and rejoice with the wife of thy youth…Let her be as the loving hind and pleasant roe; let her breasts satisfy thee at all times; and be thou ravished always with her love" Proverbs 5:1-5; 19, 20 KJV
19. It is the woman's place to cook, clean and maintain the house.	"Husbands, likewise, dwell with them with understanding, giving honor to the wife, as to the weaker vessel, and as being heirs together of the grace of life, that your prayers may not be hindered." 1 Peter 3:7 New KJV

Man's / Woman's view Point	God's Standard
20. I don't believe in student loan. I want to go to school first and you can go to school later. You also pay the bills.	"Wisdom is supreme; therefore get wisdom though it cost all you have, get understanding" Proverbs 4:7

Chapter
.3.

Marriage in a Cross Cultural Setting

Consider these quotes:
"No man was ever shot by his wife while doing the dishes"— Unknown
"I first learned the concept of non-violence in my marriage"— Gandhi
"You come to love not by finding the right person, but by seeing an imperfect person perfectly"— Sam Keen
"Love is not something you feel. It is something you do"— David Wilkerson

"A great marriage is not when the 'perfect couple' come together. It is when an imperfect couple learns to enjoy their differences"— Dave Meure

"When love beckons to you follow him, Though his ways are hard and steep. And when his wings enfold you yield to him, Though the sword hidden among his pinions may wound you. And when he speaks to you believe in him, Though his voice may shatter your dreams as the north wind lays waste the garden. For even as love crowns you so shall he crucify you. Even as he is for your growth so is he for your pruning. Even as he ascends to your height and caresses your tenderest branches that quiver in the sun, So shall he descend to your roots and shake them in their clinging to the earth......

But if in your fear you would seek only love's peace and love's pleasure, then it is better for you that you cover your nakedness and pass out of love's threshing-floor, Into the seasonless world where you shall laugh, but not all of your laughter, and weep, but not all of your tears. Love gives naught but itself and takes naught but from itself.

Love possesses not nor would it be possessed; For love is sufficient unto love. And think not you can direct the course of love, if it finds you worthy, directs your course. Love has no other desire but to fulfill itself."

But if you love and must needs have desires, let these be your desires: To melt and be like a running brook that sings its melody to the night. To know the pain of too much tenderness; To be wounded by your own understanding of love; And to bleed willingly and joyfully."
— Khalil Gibran, Le Prophète

Marriage in plain language

Some kids were gathered to celebrate their friends' birthday. The coordinator asked them some 'wired' questions. Here are a few of the questions:

What do most people do on a date?

1. Dates are for having fun, and people should use them to get to know each other. Even boys have something to say if you listen long enough. >Lynnette, age 8 (isn't she a treasure)
2. On the first date, they just tell each other lies and that usually gets them interested enough to go for a second date. >Martin, age 10

When is it okay to kiss someone?

1. When they're rich. >Pam, age 7
2. The law says you have to be eighteen, so I wouldn't want to mess with that. >Curt, age 7
3. The rule goes like this: If you kiss someone, then you should marry them and have kids with them. It's the right thing to do. >Howard, age 8

How would you make a marriage work?
Tell your wife that she looks pretty, even if she looks like a truck. >Ricky, age 10

Marriage and Cultural Considerations
The boundaries and frontiers of marriage are beyond culture and the way people live, operate and execute their daily chores. It was instituted by God and passed on to man. Generally speaking, marriage lays a foundation to how a culture should form and the tenets that guide its people if they must adhere to the teachings of their Maker. In Eden the Lord thought of creating man and woman, brought them to having fellowship with Him and Him with them. In other words, they were created for the following reasons:

- To worship their Creator together,
- For fellowship with one another,
- For warmth and procreation;
- To embrace joy and pursue happiness and
- To harness (explore, exploit and harvest) the Earth.

These five-fold 'ministries' of a family are important. To do anything contrary or even try to set the last as the first would demean the whole purpose of God as

He set out with the program of marriage. In a relationship, there must a set goal, the objective any man or woman must set before 'experimenting' the other fellow. Because man or woman is born, naturally, selfish; it takes the Holy Spirit to do a work of regeneration and re-fixing of old habits and natural traits that drive man's passion for the marriage to work according to God's plan. Culture can then come in as an embellishment, to add color and flavor to the pie. Culture is a good thing when executed with a higher authoritative source of instruction (The Bible). Because culture is dynamic and evolving, it can change given some socioeconomic shifts in people's life and/or a genre in environmental reengineering. The word of God does not change; the standard of God regarding marriage does not change also. This is why a higher authoritative source is needed; more, when the author of marriage speaks.

> "And He answered and said unto them, Have ye not read that He which made them at the beginning made them male and female; and so for this cause shall a man leave his father and mother and shall cleave to his wife and they shall be one flesh. Wherefore they are no more twain but one flesh. What therefore God hath joined together, let no man put asunder"
> Matthew 19:3-6

The original design of marriage is more than what we see today. It dates back to the beginning of time; to Genesis chapter two of the Bible. Whatever the world portends and tries to present as marriage and how family forms outside the Bible is an alteration and offense to the original blue print for marriage. I would advise for a revisit to the original script and get the information on how your marriage should work.

As a guide, try working through your marriage using this model:

Work it down from highest priority #1 to the least #5
- To worship together,

- To fellowship with your spouse,
- To come together (warmth and procreation),
- To embrace joy and pursue happiness and
- To harness (explore, exploit and harvest) the Earth.

The Other Way that Causes Pain

When a man expects his wife to act and behave like himself or where a wife usurps supreme leadership and controls the air in and around the home (courtesy of circumstances and situations that made those possible), there, the center may not hold; trouble begins. God made man and woman to mutually live together; the woman helping the man. With her virtue and glory, the wife works and supports; respects the man as her head while the man loves, curdles, appreciates such support from his wife. When any is offended, apologies stream from the heart, knowing that the primary purpose of this union is to worship together and help the other assess the presence of the Lord and in fact work your ways to heaven in the long run.

Contrary to the above model, we find many a Christian in tango with what ought to be an enjoyable, heaven-on-earth marriage. In fact it is hard to believe that a lady had a full dose of experience in her two relationships, where all turned sour and disastrous. She wrote:

"It's probably not just by chance that I'm alone. It would be very hard for a man to live with me, unless he's terribly strong. And if he's stronger than I, I'm the one who can't live with him. ... I'm neither smart nor stupid, but I don't think I'm a run-of-the-mill person. I've been in business without being a business woman, I've loved without being a woman made only for love. The two men I've loved, I think, will remember me, on earth or in heaven, because men always remember a woman who caused them concern and uneasiness. I've done my best, in regard to people and to life, without precepts, but with a taste for justice." — Coco Chanel

An African-American Cultural Mismatch

In Tennessee, an African man thought he had endured his wife for a long time; he lost his cool and killed his Registered Nurse wife and his mother in-law to death with a shot gun. According to the account, he had gone to Africa, married the girl and brought her into the US as a 'fresh green leaf'. The girl had nothing; her family could barely survive a balanced meal in a day. This man trained the wife through Nursing School without student loan while he worked real hard on odd jobs. On graduation, she wrote the board and passed as a Registered Nurse. Soon after her qualification, the real stuff she was made of came to limelight. It became one torrent of fight and rancor at home after another; one clinging fist after another, with several police calls, followed by sleep-over in police cells. After a protracted battle with the authorities at the wife's instigation, this man lost his nearly paid-off home to his wife, including the custody of his three kids to the wife. He would visit these kids just periodically according to court's order and at the discretion of the wife who sometimes comes to the appointed custody visitation location at a time of her choosing; just to 'teach the man a lesson'. He could not take it any longer. He pulled the gun as his fingers were trigger hungry, his heart engrossed with hate. The story is history with two women shot dead and the killer in death row awaiting the electric chair.

What really can explain the outrage and hate that oozed out of a man's heart towards his wife? I tend to drill back to my earlier rhyme:

"You have not seen a selfish man (woman) until you have met with one whose waking thought and sleeping meditation is on self, one who has no vision of heaven nor is given to the demanding cry of another, albeit with the intention to defraud."

Or what can explain the many divorce rates of immigrants if not for the love of money and the quest to seize the "American Dream" in a moment. Amidst cultural mix of West and Traditional Africa, many immigrants have thrown the values they came with to the winds. Ask them why: "This is America, men! I gonna do what I gonna do to be happy; to make it here in this land", they mutter. The African culture places marriage far above individual involvement. It is an extended family engagement. Family ties and bonding are so strong that it is a taboo for a man to put away his wife, except for the offense of fornication. It is heinous crime for a woman, no matter how rich, to dishonor her husband and reduce him to a mere house-help in the home. The man and his wife are cords of strong ties for the larger families, even in the face of adversity and want.

If there is famine, a man would readily move to the in-laws community to fend for a living; at least temporarily. When a woman forgets the role she was designed to play at home (to help the man, to support and respect the man) and begins to operate the program of "women liberation" (which of course underscores the fact that she was in bondage while in Africa) then you know the devil has come to judgment. The mix of cultures has created a deep divide among immigrant Christians in the West. Using Africa's values and responsibilities to impose on your spouse while the recipient gets all he/she can get without a recourse to the respect, the love and accountability that follow, according to the African custom, is an unbalanced act. Arguably, for the man to insist on a king-type authoritarian style at home is a violation of the values of his environment and of the word of God. There must be a meeting point, a place where both respect one another and combine efforts to execute projects according to the where-withal, and ability of the family. There should be a hybrid of the West and African system for African Americans; the best of both cultures in our homes and families, according to the word of God.

An Indian Overture

My colleague at work told a story of how one of us, a practicing Indian Hindu vowed not to let his kids enlist in any USA led war against any country (should the call to defend the mother land arises) because it is against Indian culture and his religion. He insists that he will choose the men his daughters will marry and that must also be according to the Hindus laws and cultures. Any violation will lead to some fracas which, we all hope, will not be at the detriment of any one fellow. My friend fails to understand that once you take the oath of allegiance to become a USA citizen, under the first amendment and the oath to defend the flag, as much as one is within the age bracket of enlisting into the army, one must necessarily bear arms to defend our new found home, the USA. It is a choice everyone seeking to become a citizen must make and live by. And talking about the choice in marriage for his daughters, my friend may even be violating the law if he imposes men on his daughters. The law has a way of nailing the naive and uninformed. All these differences in opinions and perceptions of marriage and family are coming from diverse mix of cultures, environments and upbringing which has hitherto, formed the bases of our human DNAs and thus, we have a big baggage of 'claims and rights' in defense for our actions and inactions.

I am neither a bearer of misfortune nor a prophet of doom. There is grace from above that soothes my heart and helps me to work among men despite the filth and failures of people in my generation; but I must speak out and vent myself as an averred opposition to evil. Scriptures attest that in the last days, divorce, homosexuals and all manner of evil will abound. The scripture says:

"And in that day seven women shall take hold of one man, saying, we will eat our own bread and wear our own apparel, only let us be called by thy name, to take away our reproach" Isaiah 4:1. These are happening in our time and days; or how can one explain this scenario...

In Brazil, Women shop for Husbands

Brazilian Town Run by Women Is Looking for a Few Good (Single) Men; Yahoo news reads:

"I'm sure many men have dreamed of an island completely populated by exotic women. Of course, fantasy is fantasy, but what if it were reality? In a certain regard, it is — in Noiva do Cordeiro, Brazil. It is a scenic rural town in the hills outside of

Belo Horizante with one big quirk, or perk, depending on whom you talk to. This Brazilian town is inhabited and governed almost entirely by women, its population consisting of more than 600 mostly single women aged 20 to 25. Sons are sent away at 18, and spouses are banned from the town except on weekends. Now the women have made an appeal to bring more single men to the town. But there's one caveat: Men have to follow their rules. OK, that shouldn't be too hard to do. But the truth is that any incoming men have to follow all the guidelines that the women created, from town planning to farming, religion, and more.

The motivation for the way the town is set up is a direct result of its history: The town was founded in 1891 by Maria Senhorinha de Lima, who had been excommunicated as an adulteress after leaving a man she had been forced to marry. Over time, she was joined by other single women and female-headed families, and the insular society came into being. In the 1940s, an evangelical pastor, Anisio Pereira, took one of the town's 16-year-old girls as his wife and founded a church there, imposing strict puritanical rules. When he died in 1995, the town's women determined that they would never again be subject to male domination, and they dismantled Pereira's church.

Resident Nelma Fernandes, 23, said, "The only men we single girls meet are either married or related to us. We all dream of falling in love and getting married. But we like living here and don't want to have to leave the town to find a husband." If Web traffic is any indication of interested possible suitors, it appears that the town's plea worked: Its website went down because of all the visitors to the site. So, fellas looking for an opportunity like this, you may pack your bags — Brazilian girls are calling.

Despite all these developments, I am a believer that good fortunes will sweep through the aisles and streets of our cities to bring a change that will spark off God's revival in our land. Our homes will receive lifelines as we redirect our hearts towards one another. My prayer for you is that the God of all comfort will quell all offenses and curdle you from within to forgive any and every offense. I tell people that I do not have an experience with divorce and will not have but I am careful to draw conclusions as who struck the wired arrow first; Or where the venom was first unleashed that we cannot today tame the wild beast. Whatever the situation, I want to believe that you love the Lord Jesus Christ; that you desire to see his face and live eternally with the Father. The Father says, "I hate divorce, I hate putting away." The reason for your union with your spouse is for a purpose. I understand you have worked so hard to keep the relationship, remember, someone must take the lead; to chart the course to a successful landing. It could be that God has raised you in this situation to take responsibility and save this marriage. I strongly believe in this and that is my primary purpose for writing to you: to save the marriage; to forgive and to let go, tend the home. Paul wrote to some folks who despised him:

"And He died for all that those who live should no longer live for themselves but for him who died for them and was raised again" 2 Corinthians 5:15

Chapter .4.

HOSEA BEERI & GOMER DIBLAIM: A MARRIAGE EXAMPLE

Unlike many of us preaching from the ivory towers of a Cidetal Church, Hosea (translated to mean Salvation) was a minister of mixed grill. He held a petty tent making job of a porter and grew up among his kings-men in the Northern kingdom of Israel. About the middle of the eight century B.C., soon after prophet Amos concluded his ministry, Hosea was raised by God to mention by name, a fearful and dreaded enemy of Israel, Assyria. He was a scare and terror to sin and his people whose ambits were engrossed in adulatory and spiritual harlotry. Amidst these it seemed right before God to instruct Hosea, son of Beeri to go, take a wife; an adulterous wife. Do not forget that Hosea was a no-nonsense preacher. He stood out for God and proclaimed righteousness and holiness before the people. Don't forget Hosea's environment was no different from ours today. In our day, preaching sets you aside. It connotes close relationship with God and the verity and sanctity of the accolade typifies something pristine and orderly. In certain quarters, it is a tool to amassing wealth and clearly defining your social class. It begs explaining the clout and coverage people of the 'alter' receive with the so much admired grace and glory, accompanying. Hosea and John the Baptist belong to the former class: the group that are called to step into "conflicting saga of society"; into troubled waters to tell a tale of woes and yet love the people. Such preachers stand on a hill lit with dazzling rays of light of scrutiny by the world. They must live above reproach and blame. Such was Hosea, the son of Beeri. Then God called out at him:

"... **Go, take to yourself an adulterous wife and children of unfaithfulness, because the land is guilty of the vilest adultery in departing from the Lord. So he married Gomer, daughter of Diblaim, and she conceived and bare him a son**" Hosea 1:2

This is scandalous and absurd. The preacher man married a harlot. That was God's directive. You may wonder why the Lord allowed you to get into a relation akin to Hosea: to marry someone irritable and on a parallel path. Like Gomer, some folks deride their husbands and demand for a full handsome cash provisions even if there is nothing to draw from. They are whining and complaining all the time; never satisfied, insisting on with "give me what belongs to me" demands. As I write, Luke chapter 15; a story of the prodigal son comes to mind. **"Father give me what belongs to me."** Gomer was of that breed. "Give me." She was never satisfied; going after men of different shapes and sizes, especially those with deep pockets. And yet God commands, **"...husbands love your wives...and wives obey your husbands in all things..."**

Hosea and Gomer are the two most incompatible couple I have ever seen or read, yet because of the purpose of God to be accomplished, the two were made to marry. In furtherance to the purpose of your reinstatement to the original bliss of your honey moon, I would ask you to list the differences (as per your judgment) between you and your spouse at the end of this chapter. Then we will do some asset mapping of your marriage. But do not forget that it was for the same reason in the program of God and a schedule in heaven that you got married to your original spouse. If you got it right the first time, stick to it. If not, there is abundance of mercy and pardon oozing from the throne of grace to help you. According to scriptures, the woman had married six husbands and she was heading for the seventh; the other woman was caught in the act of adultery; right in the act. She was to be stoned to death. As her accusers dragged her to Jesus, all with heavy stones to cast, Jesus asked one simple question: "if any one of you is without sin, let him cast the first stone." As He said that, He stooped, writing on the ground. I think Jesus was listing the sins of each one of the accusers. And as he raised his head, the accusers were all gone, each dropping his/her stones of offense. "Where are your accusers?" They are gone; the woman said. "I do not condemn you either, go and sin no more" Jesus said to the woman. She went home saved.

Consider again these quotes from some people I love to read:

"Coming together is a beginning; keeping together is progress; working together is success."— Henry Ford

"Aim high, but do not aim so high that you totally miss the target. What really matters is that he will love you, that he will respect you, that he will honor you, that he will be absolutely true to you, that he will give you the freedom of expression and let you fly in

the development of your own talents. He is not going to be perfect, but if he is kind and thoughtful, if he knows how to work and earn a living, if he is honest and full of faith, the chances are you will not go wrong, that you will be immensely happy." -Gordon B. Hinckley

"To say that one waits a lifetime for his soul-mate to come around is a paradox. People eventually get sick of waiting, take a chance on someone, and by the art of commitment become soul-mates, which takes a lifetime to perfect." —Criss Jami, Venus in Arms

Again let us go a little further into a relationship between Hosea and Gomer. As you read the book of Hosea, you find that they had kids, right? Gomer was always out in the night to seek for her lovers; to do the abominable thing ... and that before the eyes of the Lord. Maybe you have caught your spouse in the act. Bitter and outraged? You ought to be and that is evil in the sight of the Lord. You may have been beaten and insulted by your spouse's lover; that's also not right. Hosea had it all. I suppose as he considered divorce he was quickly reminded of God's call on his life; he must have thought about a bigger salvation awaiting Israel; his wife was before him, a ready specie of wore dorm and an exemplified Israel. The first three chapters of the Book of Hosea specifically tell us about the sin of Israel and Hosea's redemption of his wife who has gone out, 'harloting', despising her husband. As the table turned on her, she was a slave to sin, to her lovers. The midnight lovers sought for her soul, and were ready to make mince meat of her. She was to be auctioned to the highest bidder to continue to serve as a slave. God remembered His covenant with Abraham, Isaac and Jacob. There the Lord asked Hosea to go, search for and redeem his wife. As Hosea showed up, he picked the bid from the slave market; paid more than the auctioneer asked for and fully redeemed his wife back to himself. Because of his own painful experience, Hosea can feel some of the sorrows of God over sinful Israel. His love for Gomer is a reflection of God's concern for Israel. As Israel falls into the dregs of sin and is hardened against God's gracious last appeal to return, the people flagrantly violating all of God's commandments, Hosea learns the lesson why God asked him to marry Gomer; a similitude to His (God's) passion to draw Israel to Himself.

The Hosea in your Marriage

As a preacher of the gospel, it will be hard to accept to have the Hosea experience. But someone's life has been scripted out bare, for us all to learn a lesson concerning marriage and obey the instruction of God. Assuming God speaks to you saying,

"It is to the purpose of saving your spouse that I asked you to marry him/her. Do everything within your power to redeem him/her. I want to see the two of you in my kingdom above. You have my backing." What would you do?

The Lord is asking if a life is committed unto your care, by way of marriage, if you will be able to keep it. Our introductory passages indicate that there must a clear vision by everyone Christian who claims Jesus as Lord and Savior. We also indicated that we must see well enough to have a clear, succinct direction of where we are headed. Again we made it clear that given known resources heaven has left with us, courtesy of God's word and revelations of where we are going, then we can comfortably assume we know our direction and calling. May I ask,

"What is it that your couple will do that will not be forgiven under heaven if you are seeing the big picture (heaven)?

The scripture states:
"Looking unto Jesus the author and finisher of our faith; who for the joy that was set before Him endured the cross, despised the shame and is set down at the right hand of God. For consider Him that endured such contradiction of sinners against Himself, lest ye be wearied and faint in your minds. Ye have not yet resisted unto blood, striving against sin" Hebrews 12:2-4

There was a joy set before Jesus. That was the big picture. That picture drove His passion, it directed every move and quelled all offenses. As He beheld the glory, Jesus was out to accomplish His assignment; to die on the cross. I do not think it was easy for Jesus; in fact He desired that the cup should pass over Him but as He focused on the glory to come, He forgave, He prayed for His persecutors, for His executioners. Your spouse can be forgiven. You are meant for each other. There is a plea for mercy that echoes from heaven to you today. God says; FORGIVE! and reach out to him/her again. Tie the knot again; strike the original match and let the play begin.

In Merchant of Venice Portia pleads with Shylock to render mercy:

"The quality of mercy is not strain'd,
It droppeth as the gentle rain from heaven
Upon the place beneath: it is twice blest;
It blesseth him that gives and him that takes:

But mercy is above this sceptred sway;
It is enthroned in the hearts of kings,
It is an attribute to God himself;
And earthly power doth then show likest God's
When mercy seasons justice. Therefore, Jew,
Though justice be thy plea, consider this,
That, in the course of justice, none of us
Should see salvation: we do pray for mercy;

And that same prayer doth teach us all to render
The deeds of mercy. I have spoken thus much
To mitigate the justice of thy plea;
Which if thou follow, this strict court of Venice
Must needs give sentence 'gainst the merchant there."

As Portia insists that Shylock should be merciful because God is, we also notice that the notion of mercy in this Shakespeare's play has something to do with God's mandates and Christian concept of salvation. If you insist on cutting "a pound of flesh" off him/her, do not forget the other side of justice "no spilling of blood." It was for this reason that Mahatma Gandhi said:

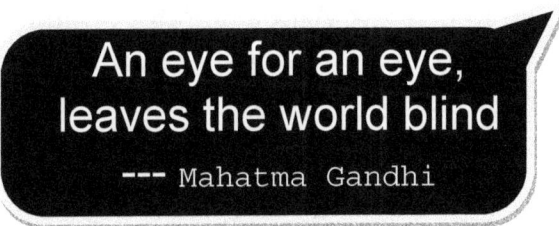

Learn to forgive and let go!

"Yes I do"

Marriage is not Contract; 'tis until death do you part!

In his book, "Isi Akwu Dara N'ala" Tony Ubesie masterfully crafted a marriage scene in a suburban town in South East Nigeria. Men and women had gathered in this big Cathedral Church for a wedding ceremony; the man and the woman looking straight into one another's eyes with acclaimed excitement. It was a society wedding because it seemed like a roll call for the 'haves' and 'have nots' of the society. I mean classy, stylish in every form. You would not be mistaken to think that it was the inauguration of President Barack Obama on February 20, 2009; but it was a wedding of rare type. As the lithology of marriage continued, the priest, conclusively said, "What God has joined together, let no man put asunder" The whole congregation echoed 'Amen' and for a moment there was silence. A mad (mentally retarded and totally disoriented) man was outside the Church Cathedral, listening; interrupted the silence and said: "man will not put asunder if they don't pull themselves apart." And I think the mentally retarded folk were right.

When you sign the register and agree to live with your spouse until death do you part; you have entered into a covenant. Here three parties are involved: God, your spouse and you. So, if you think this covenant should not hold any longer, please do yourself the good by bringing all parties involved in the covenant to the dissolution, and all the witnesses to the wedding; those who said "Amen" to the vow and prayers (dead or alive)! Even if you can pull that together, I want to ask you to drill back to conscience.

"Submitting yourselves one to another in the fear of God; Wives submit yourselves unto your own husbands as unto the Lord. For the husband is the head of the wife, even as Christ is the head of the Church and He is the savior of the body; therefore as the Church is subject to Christ, so let the wives be to their husbands in everything. Husbands, love your wives even as Christ also loved the Church and gave himself for it" Ephesians 5:21-25

The day you discover that marriage is a 'calling' and a 'work', then you will see your spouse as a work-in-progress and desire to add value to the output you already have. You will live to pray for him and desire that both of you will worship and serve the Lord despite your differences. You may need to pray for a revelation of your spouse before you throw him out or walk away from home. That man is your instrument to glory; a pointer to the fact that you are designed for glory and for beauty. The ability to hold her together and the whole family, assures heaven that you can handle the bigger Church placed under your care. You see the relevance of 1Timothy 3: verses 1 through 5. There is something men must learn: to live to please the Lord and love their wives. This is wholesome and great. Until we discover that, we may not go too far with them. However if you do go without this wisdom, observers will hear your complaints, somehow. There is a commitment we owe ourselves to the course of the family. This comes on the heels of many versions of marriage. That commitment is something worth dying for, because marriage is of God! During a meeting in Detroit Michigan on June 23, 1963, Martin King Luther said:

"There are some things so dear, some things so precious, and some things so eternally true, that they are worth dying for. And I submit to you that if a man has not discovered something that he will die for, he isn't fit to live."

Can you lay down your life for your wife? Is it possible to obey your husband in all things? Yes, these are possible if you can choose to yield to the Lord Jesus Christ and give up self and pride.

"We've been in the mountain of war. We've been in the mountain of violence. We've been in the mountain of hatred long enough. It is necessary to move on now, but only by moving out of this mountain can we move to the promised land of justice and brotherhood and the Kingdom of God. It all boils down to the fact that we must never allow ourselves to become satisfied with unattained goals. We must always maintain a kind of divine discontent." Martin Luther on Sermon at Temple Israel of Hollywood in June 1965."

Try singing a song and worshipping. That may help calm you down and do the next exercise:

Mercy Me - Beautiful

Days will come when you don't have the strength
When all you hear is you're not worth anything
Wondering if you ever could be loved
And if they truly saw your heart, they'd see too much

You're beautiful, you're beautiful
You are made for so much more than all of this
You're beautiful, you're beautiful
You are treasured, you are sacred, you are His
You're beautiful
And praying that you have the heart to fight
'Cause you are more than what is hurting you tonight
For all the lies you've held inside so long
They are nothing in the shadow of the cross
You're beautiful, you're beautiful
You are made for so much more than all of this
You're beautiful, you're beautiful
You are treasured, you are sacred, you are His

You're beautiful
Before you ever took a breath, long before the world began
Of all the wonders he possessed, there was one more precious

Of all the earth and skies above, you're the one He
madly loves
Enough to die

You're beautiful, you're beautiful
In His eyes

You're beautiful
You were meant for so much more than all of this
You're beautiful
You are treasured, you are sacred, you are His

You're beautiful, you're beautiful
You were meant for so much more than all of this
You're beautiful, you're beautiful
You are treasured, you are sacred, you are His

Exercise

List the great things you saw in your spouse during your date and engagement days:

....
....
....
....
....
....
....
....

What changed over these days/years? (Things you don't like)
....
....
....
....
....
....
....

What/Who caused these to happen?
....
....
....
....

What possible solutions do you think you hold/ can provide towards solving these issues?
....
....
....
....

Now with this list, pray, ask God for wisdom to discuss them with your spouse. Do not raise your voice or accuse him or her. Be calm!
....
....
....

....
....
....

Chapter

.5.

MONEY MATTERS & DIVORCE ISSUES

I hear many echoes from Church leaders, the pulpit and family members saying: "A feast is made for laughter, and wine maketh merry: but money answereth all things" Ecclesiastes 10:19KJV May I ask you this question from scripture also:

"From whence come wars and fighting among you; come they not hence, even of your lusts that war in your members? Ye lust, and have not: ye kill, and desire to have, and cannot obtain: ye fight and war, yet ye have not, because ye ask not. Ye ask, and receive not, because ye ask amiss, that ye may consume it upon your lusts. Ye adulterers and adulteresses, know ye not that the friendship of the world is enmity with God? whosoever therefore will be a friend of the world is the enemy of God. Do ye think that the scripture saith in vain, The spirit that dwelleth in us lusteth to envy? But he giveth more grace. Wherefore he saith, God resisteth the proud, but giveth grace unto the humble. Submit yourselves therefore to God. Resist the devil, and he will flee from you. Draw nigh to God, and he will draw nigh to you. Cleanse your hands, ye sinners; and purify your hearts, ye double minded. Be afflicted, and mourn, and weep: let your laughter be turned to mourning, and your joy to heaviness. Humble yourselves in the sight of the Lord, and he shall lift you up" James 4:1-10 (KJV)

"Deep calleth unto deep at the noise of thy waterspouts: all thy waves and thy billows are gone over me. Yet the LORD will command his loving kindness in the daytime, and in the night his song shall be with me, and my prayer unto the God of my life. I will say unto God my rock, Why hast thou forgotten me? why go I mourning because of the oppression of the enemy ? As with a sword in my bones, mine enemies reproach me; while they say daily unto me, Where is thy God? 11 Why art thou cast down, O my soul? and why art thou disquieted within me? hope thou in God: for I shall yet praise him, who is the health of my countenance, and my God" Psalm 42:7-11 (KJV)

Where it all started

Statistics show that the cause of most divorce cases has something to do with money or lack of it. It is therefore important to do the last chapter of this book on how families can manage and tame this monster. Marriage is meant for adults, not for teens or kids. Therefore in undertaking the processes of marriage we must define who an adult is in our different cultural settings. Wherever the environment is, an adult is.

"Biologically, an adult is a human being or other organism that has reached sexual maturity. In human context, the term adult additionally has meanings associated with social and legal concepts. In contrast to a "minor", a legal adult is a person who has attained the age of majority and is therefore regarded as independent, self-sufficient, and responsible."

"Human adulthood encompasses psychological adult development. Definitions of adulthood are often inconsistent and contradictory; a person may be biologically an adult, and have adult behavior but still be treated as a child if they are under the legal age of majority. Conversely, one may legally be an adult but possess none of the maturity and responsibility that may define adult character."

Wikipedia

A marriageable adult in our terms here is one who possesses the following proven and tested traits, has attained the maturity index as set by society with a sustainable plan to forge on with life. These include maturity in the area of:

- Physical and/or Bodily(Biological)
- Emotional/Mental
- Psychological/Spiritual
- Financial (ability to manage)
- Basic life sustaining instrument

So what constitutes emotional/psychological/spiritual maturity, and thus adulthood? Here are 20 defining characteristics of a true adult I found on a web site by Marc and Angel Hack Life:

1. Realizing that maturity is an ongoing process, not a state, and continuously striving for self-improvement.
2. Able to manage personal jealousy and feelings of envy.
3. Has the ability to listen to and evaluate the viewpoints of others.
4. Maintains patience and flexibility on a daily basis.
5. Accepts the fact that you can't always win, and learns from mistakes instead of whining about the outcome.

6. Does not overanalyze negative points, but instead looks for the positive points in the subject being analyzed.
7. Is able to differentiate between rational decision making and emotional impulse.
8. Understands that no skill or talent can overshadow the act of preparation.
9. Capable of managing temper and anger.
10. Keeps other people's feeling in mind and limits selfishness.
11. Being able to distinguish between 'needs' and 'wants'.
12. Shows confidence without being overly arrogant.
13. Handles pressure with self-composure.
14. Takes ownership and responsibility of personal actions.
15. Manages personal fears.
16. Able to see the various shades of grey between the extremes of black and white in every situation.
17. Accepts negative feedback as a tool for self-improvement.
18. Aware of personal insecurities and self-esteem.
19. Able to separate true love from transitory infatuation.
20. Understanding that open communication is the key to progression.

Above all, true adults do what they have to do when it is required of them, and they do what they want when they can. They are able to distinguish between the two and manage their time and efforts accordingly.

In the US, an adult is generally referred to as one who has attained the age of eighteen or above. This may not be a good answer for marriageable age. To marry, one must be mature in all the areas we have mentioned and more important, be spiritually upcoming. Because marriage is meant for men, not boys, it behooves every male who would go into this covenant to be prepared and ready. Teenagers who just got out of High School may not rush into marrying because they are not yet mature to handle the vulnerabilities of home grooming and family management.

Adam's Configuration

But when you marry, how do you keep the monster of financial face-off out of your home? Depending on the income of both couple, financial management is vital to the survival of the home. Before we get into financial management, let us take time to say that money management is not really the root cause of many problems in homes. Problems arise from the heart of folks who use money as an expression of wanton spiritual depravity. However a peep into the psychology of the man and the woman as their perception of how to manage money over and between one another is vital to a healthy relationship.

Man or woman is naturally born a cheat and a selfish person in the Adamic configuration. He/she lives to fulfill the motions of sin, self and accomplish the mandates of Satan, its master. It is therefore understandable why the old man or woman would struggle to undo the other (in whatever guise; either they live together as husband and wife or co-exist in the house as significant others); the loathe of religion, notwithstanding, the fabrics of their bonding is eaten up by greed and adamic nature. For this reason the scripture attests:

"The heart is more deceitful than anything else, and incurable--who can understand it?" Jeremiah 17:9 (Holman Christian Standard Bible)

"The human heart is the most deceitful of all things, and desperately wicked. Who really knows how bad it is?" Jeremiah 17:9 (New Living Translation Bible)

As the carnal man (flesh and self-conceited being) takes stage, the man or woman seeks to gain and rule. In the concourse of this gain-rule competition, we see husband and wife fight over money to see who takes the larger share or controls the home. The heart has not been pruned; the natural self has not been conquered by the cross of Christ and thus, SELF is on parade; fight ensures.

As we deal with the issue of money in the family, may I also submit that God made them male and female in the beginning...they were both naked and everything was open to one another as the two became one flesh. Family finances should be seen as one. It is an abnormal thing to see man running his program as the wife runs hers. Whoever the Lord chooses to be the bread winner, notwithstanding, husbands and wives must diligently seek to do the following:

1. Husbands ought to love in so far as their pay checks are an open book or at least the projects in the home are made open enough that even the wife is the supposed 'financial director' and undertakes in running the basic needs for the home; elementary considerations are known, hashed out and executed by the wife. Wives ought also to 'yield all' and surrender to the authority and supervision of the husband (if truly he is the head of the home) and provide guidance on how things should be done; including major and minor purchases.

2. In event of one enrolling to take some classes or taking a full degree program, a decision on how fees and bills will be paid should be discussed and agreed on. The situation where a man goes to Africa, marries a young girl, comes back and sends her to college (whereas he has not even attained such

education) while working some odd jobs, does not explain anything to common sense. First, the girl comes in with a mindset that "everything has been set at the king's table" and so, on graduation she starts with a salary three times more than what her husband makes. Remember, "knowledge puffeth up...of making of many books, there is no end." If that wife has not been weaned nor tamed and trimmed from inside out, she will rend the husband because she pulls the financial strings at home. The same is true for the husband who, with the help of wife married from abroad, processes the immigration papers and as soon as he gains ground in the committee of nations, decides to quit at a minor provocation.

3. Mutual respect and love should be observed by the husband and wife. Wives respect your husbands; husbands love your wives. One thing is common with wives and women in general: they believe so much in their husbands that they would want 'show off' with/about them, almost, always. They volunteer them to do the impossible and expect that they wield energies and all inertia 'just to get things done' and sometimes, to look good and be the 'nice girl' out there. By so doing you can hear them intermittently among friends talk about 'my husband' Men, real men know that in the beginning, God made them male and female; Adam and Eve, not Adam and Steve; they know that the composition of women is

different from the man, they also know that the wisdom of a man is different from the woman. A woman's preferences are different from that of a man and her care about is different also. As a man cannot carry a baby in the womb so the woman cannot carry complexities of life and process them the way a man does. Both are different. And that is according to the Maker's design and fabrication. So in all these, a woman puts up some traits alien to the man, the man ought to know that it comes from the constitution and make-up of God's design in a woman. He accepts them with love and makes a fun out of it. Life goes on.

4. Be romantic and cease from spirituality that stifles love life in the home. In managing your money, make provisions for 'couple's night out'; eating out, dating your spouse again and some fun that you know your spouse has desired for, for years. We take one another for granted and assume that 'he/she understands'. We do not understand. Love speaks, love feels, love is actionable. Decide to make active your love life again. Chuck Swindoll wrote one of the most exciting pieces: "Strike the Original Match." I think we all need to read that book as well. Let us be romantic and playful; cracking jokes and musing the other, whatever it takes.

5. Get everyone on board the family train. Cases abound where the man and his wife have some very important, but misguided intentions; executing financially laden project without the knowledge and consent of the other. Here communication is very important and transparency is the silver bullet that kills any enemy. By getting everyone involved; both will experience relief and the burden of excess loads and mistrust that goes with it, fades away. Invite the kids and show them the financial strength of the family; list the bills and commitments; and that may help in developing strategies on a way forward. On the dining table prayers will be offered in that regard. Extended family members should also know the burden on you and how much you are carrying. The extent to which you go in helping them financially depends on how well you communicate with them. Transparency here is the key word. Communication is next and third is doing your projects together (no one is left behind).

Before we turn to some exercises, may I suggest that in working out your finances, you may consult a financial planner who will help you plan, strategize and execute some instruments towards a happy and fulfilled life. As far as your family finances are concerned that will not suffice for godly counsel and prayers to support with. God ought to be at the center of the home to help you navigate through troubling waves.

I commend you to the Lord who will guide and help in these efforts to restore and rekindle love between you and your wife.

"For this reason we also, from the day we heard of it, have not ceased to pray and make [[a]special] request for you, [asking] that you may be filled with the [b]full (deep and clear) knowledge of His will in all spiritual wisdom in comprehensive insight into the ways and purposes of God] and in understanding and discernment of spiritual things—that you may walk (live and conduct yourselves) in a manner worthy of the Lord, fully pleasing to Him and [d]desiring to please Him in all things, bearing fruit in every good work and steadily growing and increasing in and by the knowledge of God [with fuller, deeper, and clearer insight, acquaintance, and recognition].We pray that you may be invigorated and strengthened with all power according to the might of His glory, [to exercise] every kind of endurance and patience (perseverance and forbearance) with joy, giving thanks to the Father, Who has qualified and made us fit to share the portion which is the inheritance of the saints (God's holy people) in the Light" Colossians 1:9-12 (Amplified Bible)

LET US DO SOME EXERCISES

Fill out this table of Income for your family

Source of Income	Husband	Wife
Biweekly/Monthly Salary		
Bonds / Share (monthly)		
Side Business Earnings		
Total Income	A	B
Less 10% Tithe + Offerings		
Net Total Income	X	Y

Let us assume X+Y = Z which is total income for the household.

    In planning your finances, care must be taken to balance the budget in order not to create confusion. The man ought to make provisions for accidentals or emergencies. Most times, he leads in major projects and capital expenditure. The woman can take care of all the details as both draw from the same purse.

Financial Management

BUDGET WORKSHEET

CATEGORY	MONTHLY BUDGET AMOUNT	MONTHLY ACTUAL AMOUNT	DIFFERENCE
INCOME:			
Wages and Bonuses			
Interest Income			
Investment Income			
Miscellaneous Income			
Income Subtotal			
INCOME TAXES WITHHELD:			
Federal Income Tax			
State and Local Income Tax			
Social Security/Medicare Tax			
Income Taxes Subtotal			
Spendable Income			
EXPENSES:			
HOME:			
Mortgage or Rent			
Homeowners/Renters Insurance			
Property Taxes			
Home Repairs/Maintenance/HOA Dues			

Home Improvements			
UTILITIES:			
Electricity			
Water and Sewer			
Natural Gas or Oil			
Telephone (Land Line, Cell)			
FOOD:			
Groceries			
Eating Out, Lunches, Snacks			
FAMILY OBLIGATIONS:			
Aging Parent's Care			
Extended Family Obligations			
Day Care, Babysitting			
HEALTH AND MEDICAL:			
Insurance (Medical, Dental, Vision)			
Unreimbursed Medical Expenses, Copays			
Fitness (Yoga, Massage, Gym)			
TRANSPORTATION:			
Car Payments			
Gasoline/Oil			
Auto Repairs/Maintenance/Fees			

Auto Insurance			
Other Transportation (tolls, bus, subway, taxis)			
DEBT PAYMENTS:			
Credit Cards			
Student Loans			
Other Loans			
ENTERTAINMENT/RECREATION:			
Cable TV/Videos/Movies			
Computer Expense/Tablets			
Hobbies			
Subscriptions and Dues			
Vacations			
CHURCH:			
Tithes			
Offerings/Gifts			
CLOTHING:			
INVESTMENTS AND SAVINGS:			
401(K) or IRA			
Stocks/Bonds/Mutual Funds			
College Fund			
Savings			
Emergency Fund			
MISCELLANEOUS:			

Toiletries, Household Products			
Gifts/Donations			
Grooming (Hair, Make-up, Other)			
Miscellaneous Expense			
Total Investments and Expenses			
Surplus or Shortage (Spendable income minus total expenses and investments)			

Wealth Creation

In meeting needs in our homes, it is important to seek professional education guidance in securing the right choice of trade, profession and whatever means of livelihood that will be used to fend for the family, positively. Such discussions on how to advance the financial threshold of a home should be held between the man and his wife.

What options are there for your family?
....
....
....
....

Assuming your wife / husband has a challenge in academics, what are the fillers out there or opportunities that you may choose to realign him/her for a real positioning?

....
....
....
....

Q2. Assuming he/she spends every dollar that he finds (whether it is credit card or cash), what do you think should be done to curtail this habit, in love?
....
....
....
....

What plans do you have for your children and retirement? Here is something to think about:

College (University Education) depending on the school and course of study is about $30,000 - 125,000 school fees alone. Multiply that by the number of kids plus housing, feeding, clothing, books and other needs. That is for one year. You may need to start an Education Fund for every child born.
      Retirement is a glorious thing that has a beginning without a good knowledge of when the end will be (until one expires, one needs to plan for the less productive, high medical expense period) The amount you are able to put away is a function of how your spending appetite allows you and the many

commitments you allow yourself to carry in your hey days of go-go life.

With all these before you, you may begin to experience agitations and present a squeezed face because there is pressure on every side arising from a little argument or disagreement. What used to be a joke is no more. The devil begins to magnify 'little nothings' into monumental details. Fun times begin to erode from the home and joy distills through the ranks of good parenting. I employ you to chill and take a break; take a deep breath and know that there is something bigger than that fuse and rancor. Because money and finance are always at the center of dis-engagements in most marriages, there is a serious concern on how money should be managed, how your wealth is managed and posted. A few points may help you through managing your money.

Wealth Management

1. Do not let other people define you or what success means to you. You must begin to create a brand called 'YOU' and do not give in to frivolities or mass selling tactics. What this means is that you must choose the things that matter most to you; to pursue a life as designed by God for you; not what peer pressure puts on you or society dictates. If you go back to yourself and your God, you will notice a very special folk, beautifully created and destined for a

purpose on Earth. You will find your companion, your spouse becoming to fulfill that desire. Sit back and find yourself, discover your niche and you will spend less out of your income. You have just begun to manage from inside your BEING. You will begin to live a life free of debt and debate in your home.

2. Put a restraint on your appetite. Consumption pattern seems to be the bane behind high profile credit card indebtedness. If you can learn to stop buying what you do not really need; 'if you can put a knife on your throat' then you will lead a happy and peaceful life with your spouse. The act of buying none essentials seem to hold back many couples down; very few times they do not realize that mere tissers at home that would ordinarily be a fun and a joke, turn soar into arguments and agitations because of financial pressure from lack of money or inability to pay bills at home. If you can learn to cut your coat according to your cloth, then you will smile again. Cut your expenses; turn away from credit card debts. They can kill your marriage!

3. Work things out together with your spouse. Plan, pray and purpose to fight the monster together. Let there be openness and truth on display. If you really mean well, if you know that you are in this marriage for good, then get together to make it work. This time, no third parties involved; get back to your

spouse and plant a kiss. If you got it wrong, apologize, if not, strike the original match and light up again. Take the initiative, swing the sling and get things started. You can be at your prime again.

Summary: First, get out of debt. Work your way to Financial freedom. Steps to financial freedom

1. Talk to your spouse
2. Figure out where you're at
3. Track your spending
4. Adjust your spending
5. Make provision for the Church & the Poor
6. Set your life goals
7. Develop a strategy
8. Review your insurance

9. Slash your taxes
10. Create an investing policy
11. Write up a will
12. Create your final plan

A research conducted by some folks in Utah provided a good insight into what God may want us to know. A majority of information following were culled from the study of families in Utah. Questionnaires were used to conduct the survey and here is an excerpt of what I found from the research.

Remembering the Good Times
When you think back on your relationship, both before you got married and after, can you think of good, positive times? When couples are going through hard times, it is common to focus on the bad and not remember the good times and good features of the relationship. But if you can recall those good times and good aspects of the relationship, then you have a better chance of being able to work through your challenges and keep your marriage together. A marriage that was built on friendship and fondness sometimes can be revived, despite the challenges you are facing now. This exercise is designed to help you try to remember the good times and good parts of your relationship

What do you remember about dating your spouse? What attracted her/him to you? What did you enjoy doing together? Write down some of your thoughts here:

....
....
....
....
....

Why did you choose to marry your spouse? What influenced you to make such a big decision to decide to spend your life together with this person? Write down your thoughts here:

....
....
....
....
....

What do you remember about your engagement? Your wedding? What are some of the positive memories from these times? Write down your thoughts here:

....
....
....
....
....

Despite your current problems, what positive things do you still see in your marriage? What good characteristics do you still see in your spouse? Write down your thoughts here:

....
....
....
....
....

Have you gone through some tough times together before? What kept you going through those times? Write down your thoughts here:

....
....
....
....
....

If you can remember some of the good features of your marriage and your spouse, it helps you to see the possibility of a better future. What have you learned by trying to remember the good times? Write down your thoughts here:

....
....
....
....
....

What factors are associated with a higher risk for divorce?

To say that nearly half of all first marriages end in divorce sounds a lot like saying marriage is just a game of chance. But a lot of research has identified various factors that are associated with a higher risk for divorce. So some people actually have a low risk of divorce while others have a high risk. Understanding these factors may not directly help you improve your marriage or make a decision about divorce, but it may help you understand why you may be facing some challenges. Of course, these factors do not guarantee that you will divorce; they simply increase your risk. Here are some factors that appear to increase the risk of divorce the most. But it is not a complete list of risk factors.

1. Young Age: Marriage at a very young age increases the likelihood of divorce, especially in the early years of marriage. Those who marry in their teens have much higher divorce rates. By about age 21 or 22, however, that risk goes down dramatically. Utahans do tend to marry young compared to the national average. The average age at first marriage for Utah is 22 for women and 23 for men. Those who delay marriage until their 20s are probably more mature and able to make better marriage decisions and handle the challenges of married life better than those who marry in their teens.

2. Limited education: Researchers have estimated that individuals who have some college education (contrary to not finishing high school) have a lower chance of divorce. Utahans are more likely to graduate from high school and get some college education than Americans in general. Apparently, investing in education is a good way to build a foundation for a better marriage, not just a better job.

3. Less income: Closely related to education is income. Researchers have estimated that individuals with annual incomes of more than $50,000 have a lower chance of divorce (compared to individuals with annual incomes less than $25,000). Finances can be stressful. Apparently having at least a modest income can help couples avoid stresses that can lead to divorce.

Increasing Your Commitment: How can you increase your commitment? One way to increase your dedication commitment is to remember the good times and all the good things you have gone through together. When you are going through hard times, it is so easy to forget these good things. Write your answer to each of these questions.

1. What attracted you to your spouse at first and then later on?

....
....
....
....
....

2. What are 2-3 of the happiest times in your marriage? Why?
....
....
....
....
....
....
....
....

3. What are 2-3 of the most difficult times in your marriage that you have been able to overcome?
....
....
....
....
....

4. What 2-3 important values do you feel you still have in common with your spouse?
....
....

....
....
....
....

5. What 2-3 important goals do you feel you still share with your spouse?
....
....
....
....
....
....
....
....
....

6. What would be the biggest loss if you got divorced?
....
....
....
....
....
....

7. What would be the biggest gain if you can stay together?

....
....
....
....
....
....

8. What three things could you do to increase your dedication commitment and show more loyalty to your spouse? Write them down here.

A..
....

B..
....

C..
....

9. With your answers to above questions, would you please, start a prayer project to God, knowing that He can fix the disconnect. The truth about your relationship is that God knows it all and He can change the heart of a man or woman. Since He was involved the day you signed up for this relationship, He can also help fix the issue. Choose a time in the night, a solitary place; alone with God.

10. Invite your spouse for a talk; a heart-to-heart discussion. You must be ready to own up; to say, "I am sorry for all the mis-steps." Be ready to a greater commitment towards the marriage. Pray with your spouse. Start the work because marriage is work.

How Common is Divorce and what are the Reasons?
1. Premarital cohabitation. Couples who live together before marriage appear to have a much higher chance of divorce if they marry. However, this risk is mostly for those who live together with more than one partner. Most only live together with one partner (whom they later marry) and these couples don't seem to be at a lot greater risk for divorce.

2. The idea that living together before marriage increases your risk for divorce goes against a lot of common beliefs that it is a good way to get to know each other better and prepare for marriage. Living together may be a way to get to know each other better, but other things about living together apparently do not help—and even hurt—your chances for a successful marriage, especially if you live together with several people before marrying. Researchers have found that those who live together already have or develop more lenient attitudes about divorce. But some researchers also think that living together may hinder building a strong commitment to each other and the importance of marriage.

3. Premarital childbearing and pregnancy. Pregnancy and childbearing prior to marriage significantly increase the likelihood of future divorce. In America, more than one-third (37%) of children are born to parents who are not married, and few of these parents eventually marry. Most of those parents will separate before the child begins school, and some will never really get together. Fortunately, Utah's rate of unwed births is one of the lowest in the nation.

4. No religious affiliation. Researchers have estimated that individuals who report belonging to some religious group have a somewhat lower chance of divorce than those who say they have no religious affiliation. And if couples share the same religious affiliation, their chances of divorce are even lower.

5. Parents' divorce. Of course, some risk factors for divorce you can't control. If you experienced the divorce of your parents, unfortunately that doubles your risk for divorce. And if your spouse also experienced his or her parents' divorce, then your risk for divorce more than triples. This is scary, but it doesn't doom your marriage to failure. It does suggest that individuals who experienced the divorce of their parents need to work even harder to make good marriage choices and to keep their marriage strong and happy.

6. Insecurity. Researchers have found that some personality factors put people at more risk for divorce. One of the most important is feeling insecure about yourself and your self-worth. Insecure individuals are more likely to become self indulging and subsequently have a feeling that the other fellow is taking advantage; or is doing much better or having a fell that he/she is deficient in some way or the other.

7. The Regret that Follows: It is interesting that a significant number of divorced individuals — maybe up to about half—report that they wished they or their ex- spouse had tried harder to work through differences. However, even feelings of insecurity and other personality characteristics can be overcome.

Further research work shows the following:
If you Quit, the Kids suffer ... for life
Studies have shown that conflict with an ex-spouse continues after divorce and adds a great deal of stress to life. Some of the new stresses include:

1. You and your ex-spouse's emotional response to the divorce (e.g., anger, retaliation, resignation, acceptance, relief).

You can outline the stress daily life chores have on you as at today.

....
....
....
....
....
....
....

If you quit, these stress levels may be multiplied but with the Lord helping, you will be able to control them. Consult a counselor for advice.

2. *My fellow worker said something that has stuck with me..."I will not consider divorce as an option, I cannot start to work on a new man; I will stay here to fix whatever is wrong and to own the process" What do you think you need to stay back and fix?*

3. What, in your opinion, are kids' reactions to Divorce?
....
....
....
....
....
....
....

Divorce generally puts children at greater risk for many kinds of problems. The problems children of divorce may experience are often present even before the divorce, perhaps the result of conflict between parents, less attention from parents, depression, or other factors. Disagreements between parents often are a gateway for children to play the umpire and gain advantage over what should ordinarily not be accepted form of behavior in homes. Children in a high-conflict marriage situation generally are hard hit if their parents decide to divorce compared to children whose parents stay married and continue to experience a family concourse and acceptance. Children in regular-conflict marriage situations, however, generally do not 'feel safe' and especially when their parents divorce compared to children whose parents stay married and keep trying to work things out. Children are developing physically, socially, emotionally, educationally, morally, and spiritually; research shows that divorce can affect children in each of these developmental areas. In adulthood, children of divorce are 2-3 times more likely to experience a divorce compared to children who did not experience a divorce growing up.

When thinking about the possibility of a divorce, one of the most important things that people think about is how divorce will affect their children.

One lady shared her experience:
"My children would cry every time Daddy left the house [while we were separating]. They would just be sobbing and crying for Daddy, and I would be holding them. And of course I wanted the marriage to work. And it was very difficult. What was difficult was to watch it hurting them and then not being able to do anything about that; to bring this pain into my children's life and not be able to stop that, because you are the guardian and caretaker of children."

According to the report from Grall, T. S. (2003) Custodial Mothers and Fathers and their Child Support: 2003 (Current Population Reports, Series P60-230). Washington, DC: U.S. Government Printing Office; In a 2008 survey of more than 2,000 California adults, two out of three divorced Californians said their divorce negatively impacted their children. It would be nice if we could provide you with a simple, straightforward answer to whether divorce will be harmful to your children. Yes, overall, good research over many years does find that children who experience the divorce of their parents are at higher risk for a wide range of negative consequences, usually two to three times the risk compared to children who do not go through a divorce. The best circumstance for children is a stable home with two parents who are happy. If an unhappy marriage can be repaired over time so that both partners can be reasonably happy, this will probably be the best situation for the children."

> *When it comes to building wealth or avoiding poverty, a stable marriage may be your most important asset.*
> —Drs. Linda J. Waite & Maggie Gallagher

Does Divorce Help Adults Become Happier?

Many studies have shown that conflict with an ex-spouse continues after divorce and adds a great deal of stress to life. Such stresses include, but not limited to;

1. Moving households.
2. Custody and visitation struggles.
3. Child support payments.
4. Financial struggles.
5. Health problems, including greater risk for abusing drugs and alcohol.
6. New romantic relationships or marriages that can bring both joys and headaches, happiness and sadness.

7. Family conflicts with ex-in-laws and other family members.

> *Divorce is a life-transforming experience. After divorce, childhood is different. Adolescence is different. Adulthood—with the decision to marry or not and have children or not—is different. Whether the outcome is good or bad, the whole trajectory of an individual's life is profoundly altered by the divorce experience.*
> *—Dr. Judith S. Wallerstein, noted divorce researcher*

The Turning Point

In concluding this little book, may I tell three stories; an eye witness version from my village. They may relate to you, they may not but at least you will learn something out of the three stories.

Story 1:
It was time when men go to farm, to cut the forest in preparation for farming. It is customary to set a day for this exercise because it is believed that the land (from the crop rotation practice, has been 'revived' or 'fallowed' for seven years) would yield it's increase. According to the ancestral trails of descents, farm lands are usually divided by our community based on clans, then into families, nucleus and extended. That year, the rich humous farmland, the lead of all rotational farms was on the table, to be divided among families. Everyone was waiting for a share of the pie because the harvest in the subsequent year, would make every farmer walk to the bank with a good return.

Two brothers from Nkem family got into some serious fuss over the ownership of their portion of farmland that lined up with the river and the other on the rocky, hilly slope (not too good). The elder and the younger were out, to go for a kill on who owns what portion. Both were armed with sharp knives (prepared for that day of clearing the forest), though issues had not been resolved. Their fumes and fists became a public specter, and as kids, we watched with excitements as they traded words and treats to kill one another. That morning was never to be created; no, not for what it brought forth through these men over a piece of farmland. Anger, hate, bitterness and all the venom one could find were freely used by these brothers. Other villagers would not leave these young men for fear of the worst happening. Some people made reconciliatory approaches but those would not appease any of the men. Remember, it was a fight to gain a better portion of the land, to have a bigger harvest and thus earn more from the returns of the farming effort. As the intensity of this duo increased, with their knives sharpened for a kill, the younger paced away from his knife, reached out for his 'snuff' (blended to powder) tobacco (usually mixed with certain caustic soda effervescent ouara that evokes sneezes on inhalation) and took a scoop of his tobacco.

Going to farm was useless if this matter was not resolved. And who owns the better portion was not a decision to come by so soon that morning. As the younger sneezed, ... and sneezed again, the elder brother rushed to him (remember the knife was not nearby), snatched the bottle of tobacco and took it by force off his hand. "Give me that snuff, stupid boy; you must not enjoy good stuff alone." He sat by him and scooped the tobacco, shoveled it into his nose and sneezed repeatedly. "Ok, let me see how two brothers will kill themselves over something that has out lived their fore fathers. With that said, both looked at each other, paused, said nothing and began to smile.

What was intended to end in a fight, was resolved with a tobacco, not a big sermon. The elder was blessed with wisdom to reach out to the younger one; he seized an opportunity and there, dissection and rancor were put to rest. Bitterness and hate can find themselves in our hearts but we must learn from the elder brother: "the land has out lived our ancestors." Freely we have received, and freely must we give. We must learn to give up the tool of offense, the substance of obstacle and use them as oyster stones to pave the path to a fulfilling marriage and home.

> The elder was blessed with wisdom to reach out to the younger one; he seized an opportunity and there dissection and rancor were put to rest. Bitterness and hate can find themselves in our hearts but we must learn from the elder brother: "the land has out lived our ancestors"

Story 2:

Mr. Okeke had taken a wife, the love of his life to the alter, at the feet of elders in my small village. He is blessed with wisdom and intelligence; a member of the village council who presided over complex issues among the people with the Eze (Chief) of our village. Along with this court house job, Okeke kept his farms and is by no means, a lazy folk. His marriage to Rita was the envy of many as people sought to be like them. The verity of home life was exemplified and their kids were indeed 'a good examle to the believers" of their time. Rita soon got into trading; buying produce during surplus seasons (likened to the communes of the Chinese perioska era); hedging them with little or no interest rates and selling off her wares during periods of scarcity or where they were in limited supply.

Mr. Okeke put down all his savings towards this trading business and he was proud of all the investments. As things turned out, Rita was beginning to blossom; making more rounds of positive turns into her produce business. It was just more than hedging or some sort of 'buying and selling'; she began to diversify; to inch in to a larger business mogul. Okeke kept his pace; maintained his statusquo as he judged at court house. His stipend was megre and the harvest from farm, very marginal. On the other hand, Rita was becoming big with deep pockets and an envy of many who knew her small beginning. Soon, somethings began to trigger off her brain. The vanity shows of life spotted her; presented themselves in style and she was quick to catch them, uncontrollably. "I am tired of this life with you as a poper; can't you be a man? Money answereth all things! Go, study that from your Bible" Rita thundered. Okeke was mute. He was a gentleman. As months passed by, Rita became more uncomfortable with Okeke since she got enough cash to buy anything money could buy; she got the media; the men who served her whims as employees and whatever she needed was at her disposal. By this time the village was beginning to take notes; everyone knew the can is filled with worms. Soon Rita was up for a game. She called the council, the Chief of the village, the press; everyone was present. She wanted to quit the marriage. According to her, she suddenly became the bread winner, bought all the things in the house since she needed to replace everything to match her taste and in fact bought the cars, the SUVs and truck for Okeke's farm business.

As she made known her case, all the hearers knew she said the truth because it was obvious that Rita was a woman of cash. She had the where-withal. Because she had cut her teeth into the juicy side of life; and almost everyone around her could feel the ooze of wealth and rich aroma of affluence. She made her case unrelentlessly without recourse to her beginning. After a rancurous ovation at her claims, the Chief then turned to Okeke; "Mr. Okeke, what do you have to say?" "Nothing" Okeke replied. Ok, Rita, gathere all your belongings and let's divide the properties. It was quick and easy. She pulled all together, everything. As her men employees were ready to start loading up, the Chief asked Okeke to go, gather any remains that could be his. Everyone knew it was a spectre of shame, a disdain to the foundation of what used to be in this home. There was nothing left for Okeke, except one thing. "I own just one thing in this life" Okeke said. "Go for it", replied the Chief. He stepped out, went straight to his wife and took her hand and declared, "I married her, I take responsibility of her. She belongs to me." And the Chief was amazed, then declared, "Case closed" Do you throw tantrums at your spouse, have you forgotten how you loved each other in the days of your youth? Your years past have paled out that it is hard to revisit your honey moon in the days of your adversity or plenty? Do not forget, in the beginning, God made them male and female... and the two were both naked.

> "I own just one thing in this life" Okeke said. "Go for it", replied the Chief. He stepped out, went straight to his wife and took her hand and declared, "I married her, I take responsibility of her. She belongs to me". And the Chief was amazed, then declared, "Case

Story 3:

It could have been a tale of woes in the wee hours of Saturday. Evangelist Neal ran to my house, pushed the button to the door bell to be let in. I knew we were not expecting a visitor that early morning and so I crept out of bed and heard for the second time, "Pastor, its me Neal. Kindly open the door." I recognized the voice and opened to receive him, though worried. "Is everything ok with you, the family and the kids?" I inquired. "Pastor, I have come this time because I respect you as my pastor; would not do anything without your knowing. I have come to my wits end. No, its all over. I mean I am done with marriage with Rose. As I go back to the house, one of us must pack and leave for the other. I am done" Neal quivered with red lips and churned face.

Truly, I have not seen Neal that angry. It was a tense and charged state of things that got him into the precipitating atmosphere. He was ready to run back to his house when sudenly I interrupted: "Neal my brother can you give me a chance before any body quits?" "No there is no remediation on this. It's over; nothing will stop parting ways with Rose" I again asked to be let in; at least, to be given a chance to talk to both, separately. After much persuation, he agreed to allow me talk to the two of them. Evangelist Neal and Mrs. Rose were married without any intention to break up along the way. Both had these "holy expectations" about the ectasies and joys marriage will bring as they were engaged to one another. Never thought it wise to engage in marriage counselling nor seek a professional counsellor to instruct them on how things go down as couples settle in their homes. The high and revered.

Expectations set in their minds must be met and executed because, "that is God's will for my life", as they both mused in their hearts. Their ego and selfish leanings had eaten deep in their psyche that both thought marriage is a 'treasure island'; a pancea for all troubles of yester-years had levied on theiir adult-hood. EXPECTATIONS! The expected and unexpected; written and unwritten all came together to haunt their relationship. Since men and women are limited in understanding and resources, there is limited provisioning and thus inability to fully express an expectation from the woman, albeit, the man.

When expectations are rife, filling the heart with what the man ought to do; what he should do and what he ought to know about me as a woman, then he (the man) strives to meet up with such or is naive about these expectations; most often, there is problem. In the heart of the woman, the man ought to know; he should have done this or that (afterall, he is the man). The same goes with the man's expectation of his wiife... she should know...; ought to do this...; does not need to be told her responsibility regarding some things... and the list goes on. These I found, constituted the bane of problems between Neal and Rose. As we talked, prayed and played back life scenarios it was obvious that we all groope like sheep without shepherd; we are all 'work in progress' masses of clay in the hands of the Porter. No clay has the right to tell the other, "you are no good, you have no place in the pile of bricks for the bigger house." Because the scripture tells us:

"Ye also, as lively stones, are built up a spiritual house, an holy priesthood, to offer up spiritual sacrifices, acceptable to God by Jesus Christ... But ye are a chosen generation, a royal priesthood, an holy nation, a peculiar people; that ye should shew forth the praises of him who hath called you out of darkness into his marvelous light; Which in time past were not a people, but are now the people of God: which had not obtained mercy, but now have obtained mercy." 1 Peter 2: 5, 9, 10

...And We can Pray

As we prayed, we cried together until there was no strength left in any of us. The good Lord began a work which He still does today. Neal and Rose are examples of a nuptial tie, unbroken, unseparatable; to the glory of God.

Would you agree with me to take up the project of marriage mending? To go the long haul and do all it takes to bring him back? to love her and curdle her to your breast? To respect him and care for him, to support him and stop the criticism? God is watching what you will do with this script in your hand. It was not for fun that this piece of information was brought to you. It was actually intended to fix the broken home and bring back smiles and joy into many families. God hates divorce:

"The Lord will cut off the man that doeth this, the master and the scholar, out of the tabernacles of Jacob, and him that offereth an offering unto the Lord of hosts. And this have ye done again, covering the altar of the Lord with tears, with weeping, and with crying out, insomuch that he regardeth not the offering any more, or receiveth it with good will at your hand. Yet ye say, Wherefore? Because the Lord hath been witness between thee and the wife of thy youth, against whom thou hast dealt treacherously: yet is she thy companion, and the wife of thy covenant. And did not he make one? Yet had he the residue of the spirit. And wherefore one? That he might seek a godly seed. Therefore take heed to your spirit, and let none deal treacherously against the wife of his youth. For the Lord, the God of Israel, saith that he hateth putting away: for one covereth violence with his garment, saith the Lord of hosts: therefore take heed to your spirit, that ye deal not treacherously" Malachi 2:12-16

Before you quit, may I request that you think back on the Cross of Jesus Christ, on the grace that streams out of the throne and a kingdom God promises to those who fight to the end. The love of Christ constrains us to do the 'foolish and despised' things in the eyes of the law and the world. Love constrains us to go the long haul. Love, oozing from Calvary, compels a man or woman to think beyond immediate solace and enrichments that divorce brings. The more I think about these, the more I understand why ministry and public life are tired to how well a man manages his home; how the rich content of his/her family offerings define or determine how far he/she goes and is sustained. As you drop this book, can you pray a soul searching prayer to God to keep your marriage from disintegrating; to keep you closer than before to your spouse; to do things together and behold the face of the Lord Jesus at His appearing. Go, in this might. And may the grace given for marriage at Eden; the strength and vigor provided on the day you said, "Yes I do" be renewed and revitalized in your inner man.

May the God of all peace be to you a guarding and guiding Light in your thoughtful decision in life; may help come to you from above and favor from men to help navigate the tortuous waters of society and life; to the end that you will come out the way God intended it for you.

Jesus said; "...but in the beginning it was not so..." May He who inhabits the universe cover you from shame of divorce. May the Lord institutionalize the very blue prints of marriage in our society and bring back sanity and sanctify the ordinance thereof, helping men and women not to do the very things dogs and cats despise. May the Lord grant us understanding and wisdom to know that our spouses are in the same heavenly race as we are, under the same depraved world system; that a day comes when, beyond the horizon, on the other side of eternity, we will understand ourselves completely with all errors unveiled. Then we will lift our hands in praise to the Father for the grace to bear one another with long-suffering. May the trust bestowed on us as custodians of the faith not be traded for frivolities of the present; may the envy of Angels on us be sustained and kept intact until that day of testimony when we will be surrounded by a legion of the host of heaven in a town hall meeting as they ask us; "how was your Earthly experience", "tell us how you strove against the Tempter who made all attempts to scatter your home, even at the gravest offense?"

As you pray, I commend you to the Lord to keep you from falling; to keep you from failing; to give you strength and vigor from the inside, in your inner man; to make a permanent in-print in your heart that you are in this marriage for good; that you may make an unbending resolve NEVER to quit. Amen!

REFERENCES

APA, and homosexuality; The seventh edition of DSM-II, 1974
Philip Hickey, "Homosexuality: The Mental Illness That Went Away"
Dr. Ferdinand Nweke "UNDERSTANDING LIFE" Study Course from Eternity Ministries
    Yahoo news; www.yahoo.com
        Emmanuel Elendu "Personal Discipleship"
        Emmanuel Elendu "Digging for Gold"
    Chuck Swindoll "Strike the Original Match"

Select Bibliography
Harlan, Lindsey, ed. From the Margins of Hindu Marriage: Essays on Gender, Religion, and culture. New York: Oxford University Press, 1995.
Kannan, Chirayil. Intercaste and inter-community marriages in India. Bombay: Allied Publishers, 1963.
Manning, Henry Edward. Indian Child Marriages. London: New Review, 1890.
Uberoi, Patricia, ed. Family, Kinship, and Marriage in India. New York: Oxford University Press, 1993.

About The Author

Emmanuel Elendu was an Investment Analyst; then a Financial Reporter. He moved from Commodity Trading to Textile Importation where he worked as an African Representative for a UK firm. He combined business and ministry; planted Churches as a missionary in Nigeria, Kenya, Malawi and South Africa. Since 1982 he served under Scripture Union, Christian Union, NIFES, Christian Pentecostal Mission and The Redeemed Christian Church of God.

He published "Commodity Map of Nigeria" (1998), an investment finder that helps with resources repositories of hard and soft commodities. In 2012, he published "He got me Jazzed and Inspired" a training manual for School of Disciples. Emmanuel is the founding Pastor of RCCG Dominion Centers in Cincinnati and Dayton Ohio; and Northern Kentucky. He is a consultant in Information Technology. He brings a rare combination of corporate life with scriptural insights that exemplify the man on the street fitting into the principles and practice of the Kingdom of God. His simple, 'out-of-the-box' and practical approach to ministry is intriguing; lending to the books, "Digging for Gold" and "Before You Quit."

Other Books by Emmanuel Elendu

Personal Discipleship
Before You Quit
Digging for Gold
He Got Me Jazzed & Inspired

www.ingramcontent.com/pod-product-compliance
Lightning Source LLC
Chambersburg PA
CBHW070455100426
42743CB00010B/1635